Praise for Wayne Stier

"*Stars When the Sun Shines* reminds us to live our lives with gratitude, grace, and appreciation. Balanced by the bittersweet reminder that our time here is finite, Wayne's story is both courageous and poignant, a lifetime in the making."
　　—Alison Wright, author of *Learning to Breathe: One Woman's Journey of Spirit and Survival*

"With startling detail, humor, and a poet's heart, Wayne Stier faces his death by gloriously living his life. He travels the world with his wife, visits ancient caves, teaches, writes, learns from wise elders and reminds all of us to focus on what truly matters."
　　—Louise Nayer, author of *Burned: A Memoir*

"*Stars When the Sun Shines* is an offbeat, upbeat, oddball, goofy, loose-limbed human comedy of a book. Wayne Stier's life and times reads like a Kurt Vonnegut novel."
　　—Gary Leon Hill, playwright, author of *People Who Don't Know They're Dead*

"In reading *Stars When the Sun Shines,* I realized that we search for the rightful cause of our death throughout all of our life—until it comes to us as a recognition of our own first cause. Then, finally, our spirit can burst forth into total acceptance of our life."
　　—Joy Nemiroff, astrologer

"Wayne showed us in his last days on earth how to truly embrace life: by spreading wide his arms, radiating compassion, dignity, acceptance, and above all, love."
　　—Keiko Abe-Ford, author and founder and president of Communication and Language Associates

"I loved *Stars When the Sun Shines*. It is written with truth. Laughing at death, Wayne finds his way to Asia and takes you from one hilarious episode to the next. He lived his life by conquering his fears with love."

—Ginny Holt, photographer collaborating with writer John Holt on *Coyote Nowhere* and *Arctic Aurora*

"It is no surprise that my friend Wayne would manage to sing duets with the surgeon who removed his left foot, attend his own funeral, and as was his habit, embrace it all. His ultimate forgiveness of self and others led him to a temple deep in a forest of love-consciousness. Thank you for sharing your star path, traveled hand-in-hand with Mars. May many follow your loving lead."

—Jim Ford, family therapist and human development research scientist at the University of Georgia

"As unbelievable Wayne's stories may sound, I know they are true, for I am one of the lucky people whose lives intersected with his—in Malacca, Flores, Koh Phangan, and Hawaii. I learned a lot of important stuff along the way: how to really travel, how to play cribbage in an over-crowded minibus while traversing a mountain range, how to write better, how to enjoy the stars on an island beach at night. *Stars When the Sun Shines* is his masterpiece: the inspirational odyssey of one of the quirkiest human beings it has been my privilege to know."

—Margaret Sarkissian, ethnomusicologist, author of *D'Albuquerque's Children: Performing Tradition in Malaysia's Portuguese Settlement*

"Anyone having trouble dealing with a physical affliction in his or her own life would do well to read this book and see how one man coped. Stier steadfastly refused to take himself too seriously, even when he knew his days were numbered."

—Scott Berry, author of *A Stranger in Tibet: The Adventures of a Wandering Zen Monk*

Stars When the Sun Shines

Also by Wayne Stier:

Wide Eyes in Burma and Thailand: Finding Your Way

Hawaii Blue

Malacca Gold

Time Travel in the Malay Crescent

Stars
when
the
Sun Shines

A MEMOIR

WAYNE STIER

WEISERBOOKS
San Francisco, CA / Newburyport, MA

First published in 2010 by
Red Wheel/Weiser, LLC
With offices at:
500 Third Street, Suite 230
San Francisco, CA 94107
www.redwheelweiser.com

Library of Congress Cataloging-in-Publication Data
Stier, Wayne.
  Stars when the sun shines : a memoir / Wayne Stier.
    p. cm.
  ISBN 978-1-57863-473-6 (alk. paper)
  1. Stier, Wayne. 2. Stier, Wayne—Health. 3. Authors,
American—Biography. 4. Stier, Wayne—Travel—East Asia. 5. Travel
writers—United States—Biography. 6. Cancer—Patients—United
States—Biography. 7. Radiotherapy—Complications—Case studies. 8.
Pain—Psychological aspects—Case studies. 9. Foot—Amputation—Case
studies. I. Title.
CT275.S727A3 2010
910.4092—dc22
  [B]

                                2009045550

Cover design by Stewart Williams
Typeset in Perpetua and Futura
Cover illustration © Wayne Stier

Printed in Canada
FR
10 9 8 7 6 5 4 3 2 1
The paper used in this publication meets the minimum requirements of the
American National Standard for Information Sciences—Permanence of Paper
for Printed Library Materials Z39.48-1992 (R1997).

Contents

....

I remember lying on my back as an infant in the pillowless crib. I would swing my head back and forth, from side to side, picking up speed and rocking myself to sleep. For me, when other people were rocking, it never lasted as long as I liked.

Myth of the Wagon Star

....

I AM BEGINNING TO SEE THAT whatever happens in my life, your life—in everybody's life—is part of a cosmic plan in which we are participants if we choose to be. One can see the plan more clearly if one looks upon one's life as a myth.

A myth is a story that explains a phenomenon usually involving supernatural beings or events. This myth of the Wagon Star is a ride offered to you: the transmutation from our present third-dimensionality into the fifth dimension of *love-consciousness*. This shift has already begun for many of you. The gate is opening now. The wagon is going through. Hop on if you like, and be welcome.

The Wagon Star myth unfolds—or, more accurately, blossoms—in a place outside of time. Most of it appears to have been written over a period of three weeks. I rode the story rather than wrote it, and only near the end did I discover where I was being carried.

The language of this book is metaphorical rather than literal. Metaphor is different than fiction. Metaphors draw relationships between people and things; they connect on a different level, on different dimensions. The myth of my life is a metaphor for yours.

All the events you read here happened to me, as unbelievable as they may appear at first. There is no fiction or exaggeration in what is told. You will soon find out why I feel this disclaimer necessary. I ask you to trust your heart. A red thread winds its way through the whole tapestry of events. It is a wild and often hilarious ride around the planet to . . . I can't start at the end of the ride. Let's back up at least to the middle, to the muddle, before we get to the beginning.

......

When I moved to Hawaii the first time, in December 1983, I drove into Hale Halawai parking lot to have a close-up look at the ocean. Three large Hawaiian *moke* got out of my rental.

"*Alo ah*," I said, nervously.

One of them spat and looked out to sea. Another rolled his eyes. The third turned up the volume on his sneer. "'*Alo ah.*' Geez. *Haole* Pidgin. It's alo *ha,* brah. *Ha.* Put some breath into it, like you mean it. And try some smiling," he barked ironically. "What you doin' on my island? You just tryin'."

"Of course I'm tryin'. You guys are big."

What was I doing on his island? Why did I think I had the right to share paradise? To him I was just another stranger taking more and leaving less. As corny as it may sound, I asked the stars for a sign. I think maybe I saw someone do this in a movie. I waited. No answer.

Someone once asked me if Wayne Stier is a nom de plume—the name of my quill, my feather name. Who in their right mind would choose this for their name? No offense to my folks or ancestors, but as a pen name chosen over any other? Wayne Stier? Get real.

At that time I didn't know the impossible coincidence, the profound synchronicity, the magic that rests in the metaphor of my name.

Wayne means "wagon." The wainwright makes wagons. *Stier* sounds like "steer." It is German for "bull" but has lost something in the translation. In the Nordic languages, however, *stier* means "star." The starboard of the ship came from the Norwegian word *stierboard.*

The Big Dipper is called Charles's *wagon,* after Charlemagne. It is also known as the wagon of King Arthur. If you follow the arc of the Big Dipper's handle across the sky, you will come to Arcturus, the giant golden star a mere 43.9 light-years from earth. (A light-year is six trillion miles.) It is as if the star is pulling the wagon. *Arcturus is the wagon star, or the Wayne Stier.*

Since the Big Dipper is King Arthur's wagon, it would stand to reason that the star Arcturus must represent one of the knights of the Round Table. Which one is Wayne? Sir Gawain would be the obvious choice. Who was Sir Gawain?

......

They played a rough game in the court of King Arthur, where after a hearty feast one of the knights would challenge anyone who dared to a duel: "Hit me as hard as you can and I'll take it. Then I'll hit you as hard as I can. Take it if you can. We will see who stands the longest."

For the Green Knight this was a sissy game. He wanted to see if there was any truly brave knight in the court willing to wage his honor against his life. Sir Green had Morgan le Fay sprinkle him with a charm that protected him from death.

On Christmas Day the Green Knight, whose real name was Bredbeddle, steps forward with a challenge: "Anyone may choose any weapon and have the first blow at me on the condition that in a year and a day you meet me at the Green Chapel for me to return the blow."

Everyone laughs nervously, but no one rises to the challenge. Finally, exasperated that none of his "brave" knights are willing to accept the duel, King Arthur begins to stand. Gawain jumps up quickly so that his king can save face. He chooses a battle-ax and with one mighty blow severs the Green Knight's head from his body.

Sir Green calmly picks up his severed head and tucks it under his arm, laughing. "See you in a year and a day," he says.

Gawain's life is now totally changed. Everything he does for that entire year, every moment, will be done with a consciousness that had not previously been there. Each act he performs now had grown more important. Everything has become a metaphor for life once death has become a certainty.

On the appointed day Sir Gawain goes to the Green Chapel as honor demands. Sir Green Bredbeddle is sharpening his blade when Gawain arrives. Gawain puts his head on the chopping block. Sir G.B. takes a swing and misses. Gawain remains with his head on the block. Again G.B. swings and misses. Again Gawain remains on the block. Bredbeddle promises that the third one will not miss, and it doesn't, barely nicking the skin on the side of the unflinching bared neck. The Green Knight bows deeply with respect in the presence of such loyalty and bravery.

From that time forward, Sir Gawain became one of the most powerful knights in the court of King Arthur.

I identify with Sir Gawain. He wasn't really brave, but didn't want to be identified as a coward. He knew he was dying and that made his life more meaningful. As for the details of my personal story, old Bredbeddle nicked me with his ax with his first swing at my right knee. My second time to the hospital, for cancer, changed my life, and the third swing of the ax cut my legs from underneath me.

......

The star that the Polynesians followed to find the Hawaiian Islands, the one they call *Hokule'a,* or "Star of Gladness," is Arcturus. My name, I discover, is the sign I requested a quarter century ago. Wayne Stier and the Star of Gladness are the same. The star is directly overhead on the Island of Hawaii at South Point, where in July 1998 my wife, Mars, and I decided, seemingly by chance, to build our home. Considering how much I have zigzagged around this planet, this is yet another miracle. It's as if the star were a metaphor for me, and vice versa.

The man in the mirror winks
First on my right, the left eye,
Then on the left, his right eye,
Then both eyes at once, I think.
I think.

My middle name is Otto. Fortunately, I'm dyslexic. There is an odd sort of symmetry even in this. To have been given a name that would cause a dyslexic no problem seems unusually prescient, even for my parents. Or do you believe in coincidence?

Stars When the Sun Shines

My mind functions differently than the average person's, I think, judging from incongruities that often arise in conversations. Imagine seeing things—everything, not just words—in a mirror. This metaphor limps. My thought process is more akin to turning a tennis ball inside out without cutting it. There is no ordinary vocabulary available for this mind-set. Let me show you instead.

The next time you watch the sun set, you might want to sit down. You can feel the world moving a thousand miles per hour, and you are going backward.

Try another thought. If you shine only green light on a plant, it will soon wither. It reflects green, having no use for that color. So what we call green grass is actually every color but green. The sky is every color but blue. This is comforting to a mind like mine.

Sometimes thinking inside the mirror gives you a completely new reality. The sky as viewed from high on the slopes of Mauna Loa in Hawaii on a clear moonless night is clustered with so many stars, you can actually see the clouds where the stars aren't. Think about it. I am not talking nonsense. If you look at a sky filled with stars and find a place where no stars can be seen, that isn't a hole in the sky. It's a cloud.

At the top of Mauna Loa when the sun shines on the frost and melts it, the frost remains unthawed gray-white in the shadows beside the dark black wet rock exposed to the sun. The world turns into a black-and-white photo negative of itself.

Myth of the Wagon Star

Silence is the space between dog barks. Just listen to it. You could think of a dog's bark as a dot pointing out the silence. It is possible to make that choice.

How do you know that there aren't other dimensions happening at this moment if you haven't seen any traces? And if there are other dimensions, we most certainly are in them now. All we need to do is become aware of the leaks between these dimensions. Stars fill the sky even when the sun shines, after all.

For us everything is thought. If it isn't thought, it doesn't exist. If it exists outside of our thoughts, how could we know, and what would it mean to us?

My dad once asked me if I believed that people were going to understand my writing. He knew me, thought he understood, but wasn't sure. I agreed that it might be a problem. I didn't know if I could possibly communicate reality as I see it. "I guess people are going to wade in as deep as they want," I said, "but if someone is ready for a swim, it would be a shame if they were to keep hitting bottom."

We saw the world differently. He took the world seriously and found me flippant. He tried to instill humility in me.

> One day my father said to me,
> "How natural, humility."
> Whenever father gazes down
> From the summit of a mount
> At the expansiveness, he sees
> How insignificant is he.

Stars When the Sun Shines

......

I understand what he is saying,
But that is not the game I'm playing.
For when I on some summit stand
Surveying the vast and rolling land
Humility is not inspired.
The hill has grown 'bout six feet higher.

I had no way of knowing if anyone shared my existence. If all is thought, who is thinking all this? Am I just making things up?

This state of being is called solipsism. I felt as if I were a bubble of existence in a lonely sea of whatever. There is a humorous story of a woman who wrote to the philosopher Bertram Russell: "After reading your book I am relieved to discover that you are a solipsist, too."

It doesn't work that way. Rather, the bubble of my existence slowly hardened into a shining silvery ball bearing with an empty, hollow center.

Pinball Wizard

APRIL FOOLS, 1971. The pinball wizard pulls the spring-loaded plunger, shoots the silver ball, and the game of Pull the Wagon—Wayne Stier—begins. For reasons that will make sense eventually but did not when they were happening, Mars, my wife of three years, had a car accident, sliding on ice into a frozen meat truck. She took a big bite of the steering wheel. When I arrived at the hospital, she was on a gurney, waiting for surgery. Her sliced bottom lip was hanging open. She was toothless. I was near fainting. She motioned for me to come closer and said as best she could, "Wayne, cancel my beauty appointment."

I was losing the only person I ever knew who understood my soul. We found out later that had she hit the unpadded steering wheel anywhere other than at her breakaway teeth, the blow would have killed her. We didn't feel grateful at the time. I was bitter and swallowed my anger as a time-release poison pill.

Two years later I took a routine physical for my first teaching position, in Coon Rapids, Iowa. The doctor suspected I had a tumor and suggested exploratory surgery. This entailed the removal of my left testicle—not pleasant for a person with a name that sounds like *steer*. The test came back positively malign. I returned for a full gut opening, where the doc picked out my troublesome lymph nodes as if he were harvesting grapes. The last one, up in my chest as high as they could reach, was found to be malignant.

Before the doc operated, he told me that it was not easy to tell my lymph nodes from the ganglia that controlled the flow of sperm. I suggested he wear new glasses. It didn't help. I had been surgically removed from the physical history of humanity, a cul-de-sac of a breeding human being. Mars and I bonded on a spiritual level. She was content to live without children of our own, despite the fact that the burden would fall entirely on her when I die.

I needed to have radiation five days a week. We would leave school early—I'd skip out of monitoring study hall—and drive to Des Moines, an hour away, go for my thirty-second dose in a room that smelled to me of burnt flesh and lipstick and then return home, arriving after dark. It was exhausting. Mars did all of the driving. She also quit wearing lipstick.

After three months of numbing radiation, they looked at my blood count a final time and, because I was young and otherwise very fit, gave me a fifty-fifty chance to live. I felt that the doctor was lying to help me handle the really bad news. I left without a thank-you. I never wanted to see a doctor again in my life. A flip of the coin, and I wasn't feeling lucky. My name was turning ironically negative. Wayne: to become lesser, as in the *waning* moon. Stier: as in a castrated bull.

Still young, this already was my second trip to the hospital. The first was in October 1962, when I was fifteen. I had to have the cartilage in my right knee removed—a high school football injury that broke my heart. I loved the game, loved to play it full out. Ironically, this injury occurred during a half-speed drill, the last one I would ever participate in. I was following instructions at that time. This has become progressively more difficult for me.

Before the operation I was given a local anesthetic, a long needle full of fluid stuck into the base of my spinal cord. As the fluid to kill the pain is slowly oozed into my nerve system, the process continues to be very painful—but only until the needle is removed.

Pinball Wizard

A nurse-accountant ran in and demanded that we go no further, nor could we remove the needle, until they had obtained a waiver from my father. It was an eternity before that needle was removed. I was sweating from the pain. All that pain so that they couldn't be sued? "Jesus loves me, this I know. But those doctor so-and-so's."

I was filled with self-pity about my bad luck at having to experience that screwed-up operation so young. I remember rolling down the hospital hallway in a wheelchair chasing after nurses for the impotent fun of it when an elderly man called out from a room I was passing and invited me in.

He asked me how long I was in for. "It will be five days before I finally get out," I complained. "How about you?"

He smiled. "I have lived in a hospital for most of the last twenty-eight years."

"That sucks. So why are you smiling?"

"When you realize what a precious gift life is, son, you will see only joy." His face showed me he meant everything he was saying. I thought he was delusional. He was the happiest man I had ever met. It confused me that someone who had such a great reason to complain was so content.

"Sure, I guess. But twenty-eight years?"

......

The knee operation was only minimally successful. My leg kept slipping out of joint at times ever afterward. I was so angry with the doctor for leaving in me something around which grew a golf ball of a calcium deposit that I stole his reflex hammer from him. I hated all doctors.

Still, I had some speed if not lateral movement, so I played defensive noseguard, always going full out straight ahead. I loved it. When I went to college I was a walk-on for the junior varsity. I felt I needed to bang my body around to get ideas to seep into my brain. Every day at practice the trainer applied three rolls of tape to that knee. Every week I spent ten hours in the hot tub to bring down the swelling. I reached the conclusion halfway through the season that it wasn't going to get any better. The day I went to the coaches' office to quit, I found out I had been promoted to varsity. I couldn't refuse, and I accepted the pain as the price for the privilege of playing.

I was the only poet-philosopher on the team. This surprised me. I guess I was out of touch with what most people thought was obvious. I didn't play football only with my body. I would watch the opponents, look them in the eye, study their body language, and predict where the play would go. I usually guessed correct.

I lasted on the team the rest of that season and stayed with them as a respected ball boy. Then in the summer of 1967, I met Mars. We were on the same team selling encyclopedias door-to-door, slogging books and dodging Green River laws and the anti-peddling police. We became engaged after two months.

It surprised me, too. We were in the middle of a heated philosophical argument. To anyone who didn't know any better, it would probably have sounded like a quarrel. I felt she was stubborn. In the middle of my anger, I heard a voice: "You should marry this woman." I was still angry, but somehow the disagreement disappeared. It made no sense to me at all, but I couldn't explain the voice, so I asked her to marry me. I didn't know if I loved her. I thought I did. Can one think one loves someone?

The advice from the voice was perfect. We were married in July 1968. I was twenty-one; Mars, twenty. We are still married, happy together—and together even when we are apart—for over forty years now. Amazing.

I dropped out of college to work selling wood paneling to home-remodeling dudes who wanted a basement sports bar. During slow times I would stare at the wood grain and imagine I saw images.

"Wayne. Wayne. Come back here. You're daydreaming again."

"Customers waiting, Stier."

Lost my college deferment and was drafted to be sent to Vietnam. The man at the final desk paused, his stamp in air, ready to come down like a hot brand on a calf's butt, when he noticed my mention of knee surgery. He frowned and called me a draft dodger, but he wrote out a slip and sent me to the vets' hospital to have my knee x-rayed. "Then we'll get your sorry ass to 'Nam."

At the Vets, Doc comes out with a grim face: "Got some bad news for you, boy. You are never going to make it as a soldier with that knee. You get it fixed, and we will get you in."

"Gee, Doc. I can't tell you how bad that makes me feel."

The knee has never been fixed.

I went back and finished college, mostly through independent study. Some of the classes I was even allowed to design myself following my personal interests. And I continued on in a program for a master's in the Art of Teaching.

I had to drop out again after Mars's accident. We were without an income. We took a job at the Bar None Ranch in Anoka, MN as houseparents for six emotionally disturbed children aged nine to fourteen. They were just normal kids reacting to an abnormal environment. I could identify. But it soon evolved into a job as a jailer. Punishment. Reward. This is how we train dogs.

In order to get my group to function maximally without constant supervision, I read the college course book on group dynamics about rewarding each person in a group for taking on their natural function, be it clown or leader, doer, or group conscience. I convinced my professor, Dr. Evans, to allow me to take the course, Independent Study in Group Dynamics (I love the sound of that), using our six kids as a test for the theory.

It worked. Ours was the only group at the Bar None Ranch that functioned well when not supervised. With that course I completed my master's degree.

Pinball Wizard

I had passed my final exam the previous fall by accident. As was my wont, I was talking intensely to a fellow student I met in the hallway. He was on his way to something important. It was his final exam for the master's course. It showed in his face. He was slightly relieved to be distracted. When he walked into the test room, I followed and sat beside him, continuing the thought I was chasing. I had planned to leave when the test started.

The tester, a friend of mine named Dr. Dorothy Evans, noticed that I wasn't on the list, but she told me that I would be allowed to take the test if I really wanted to. I asked what would happen if I failed. She told me I could take it again in the spring. So, with nothing to lose, I took my final and passed it with absolutely no additional study.

I applied to fifty high schools without an answer. No one wanted to pay a master's salary to a beginning teacher. Finally I got an interview at Coon Rapids, Iowa. It seems they had a slot for a combination English teacher and assistant football coach. If I hadn't played football I would never have landed the job.

The superintendent came rushing into his office for our appointment and apologized: "Sorry I am a little late."

"You are fifteen minutes late, but that's OK. You are hiring me. I am not hiring you."

I missed the first two weeks of my teaching career, using all my sick leave to recover from the cancer operation. After the operation I intended to bounce back super fast, and did so by most standards. Rule of slapstick: stand up quick, and pretend it didn't happen.

At the old brick school building I had to use the handrail to pull myself up to my third-floor room. I was on some pain drug that made me weird—or, just as likely, more normal. I used coffee to stay awake.

To my students: "I have cancer, and I've got some good news for you. We are all going to die someday. So let's not waste the time we have left. If we aren't enjoying what we're doing, let's find a way to do so."

I guaranteed them that literature was not a punishment. They laughed me out of the room when I told them it was better than TV.

The radiation caused me to have the urgent need of a bathroom at odd or awkward moments. Even as we traveled around the world, I rarely had more than a fifteen-minute warning before my bowel situation became dire. Put that on a thirteen-hour bus ride and you have reason for concern. I informed my students that they had their teacher's career in their hands. We made a fairness treaty. There was never a problem when I was out of the room—until I became stronger, that is.

The principal was another matter. He came into my classroom scowling one day and scolded me in front of the ninth-graders for a textbook one of them had dropped in the alley. I asked him to please leave. I would talk with him later.

Pinball Wizard

In his office I told him that if he entered my room again, no matter what the reason, the class would belong to him. I'd be gone. Life was too short for me to take that kind of—I used a word then that I would prefer not to use now. Saying that to the principal felt good.

He never appeared in my classroom again. Instead, he tried to use the intercom to spy on me, but unfortunately for him it made a static noise. I would switch midsentence into a lecture about the dangers of Big Brother. Some of the ninth-graders were in on the joke and started reading *1984* and asking intelligent questions to fool the principal.

By the following spring of 1974 Mars was bored to tears. She decided to start up a community theater group in a town of only thirteen hundred people. Fat chance, that. Only one person showed up to help choose the play, so I volunteered to read a couple of the parts. I did it as a favor to Mars. I didn't want to be the one that caused her dream to fail after all I had put her through. I made it clear to her that there was no way she was going to get me onstage.

At the reading, I played the first part with a very overdone imitation of John Wayne and for contrast chose an effeminate voice for the other character, Richard. I was cast in the latter role, which was to be played exactly as I had misread it. Despite my firm objections, shored up by an extreme fear of the stage, I found myself strutting across the boards as a girly man. The play, *Blithe Spirit*, by Noël Coward, was performed in the same building that had been the dressing room for the previous fall's 0–8 football season, during which I had acted as assistant coach. Talk about identity issues. (Come to think of it, I was not asked to be the coach the following year.)

I stole the show. In the audience was Roswell Garst, the Iowa farmer who brought Khrushchev to his pig farm in 1959. He laughed loudly through a hole in his neck amplified by a vibrator. For months after, whenever I met someone downtown, even if they were across the street they would inevitably wave at me limp wristed in an overdone imitation of my Richard. That farmers' town began to prance around as a gaggle of ersatz gays. At parties they asked for Richard rather than Wayne, and I could stay in character as long as I wanted. (I wish to apologize to all gay people for having made them into a joke. I played the part with feminine dignity, but the audience saw it as ridicule. I wasn't conscious of this at the time.) I was happy that people were laughing at my illusion. I didn't feel quite so alone.

Meanwhile, I felt my precious time slipping away. I began to toy with the idea of writing a country and western song. (*"I'll get by with killing time, till time gets 'round to killing me."*) Only thing was, I didn't know how to write music. (What Miss Wiggins tried to teach me was how to play other people's music.)

I vowed to live my life to the fullest, but here I was in small-town Iowa teaching high school English. Do

Pinball Wizard

21

you see a headliner here? Neither could I. I wanted to live every moment, to squeeze every drop of life from each day. My ideal was an anecdote I had read about a French bishop.

We all are going to die someday. So what?
Bishop's playing cards. His flock is shocked.
"If you were to die five minutes nigh
You'd pray now would you not?"
"I'd play this hand. You see the hand I got!"

Looking at my hand, the only way I could possibly win was to bluff. How do you bluff a flip of the coin? The illusions onstage were as real to me as anything else. I wished they were more real.

Unhappy in small-town Iowa, we moved to a much larger small town, Charles City, Iowa, with a very active community theater.

I had the lead in *The Last of the Red Hot Lovers,* my seventeenth play in three years. The irony had not escaped me, for I was able to perform sexually with only the echo of feeling and no ejaculation. I felt that I was wasting what little life I had left. Once again, as always, the comforting illusion of the stage had disappeared. I was in that dreaded space between plays. My fear of dying had blossomed into anger at the unfairness of life.

"'Now is the winter of our discontent,' *Richard III,*" I enunciated theatrically. I was drunk. My bum was freezing from sitting in the snow. *Perhaps I could freeze to death,* I thought sardonically. Death by frozen gluteus maximus.

I shouted at the stars, *"Get me out of here!"* My friend Larry coaxed me back inside.

My self-esteem was at its nadir.

How stupid of God to make me,
When He / She does most things right.
It must be presumptuous to tell She or He,
"I'm afraid that you had an off night."

The next morning Larry drove over to my house with his Sunday newspaper. He had circled a job opening for a college theater director and thought I should apply. I would not have been deemed qualified by academe to be a professor of drama in college, for I had taken but a single drama course, and that as an independent study.

......

I needed one drama course to be certified to teach English in high school. It was two years after I graduated from Wartburg College, December 1969. I called my mentor, Professor Sam Michaelson, and asked him if he could help. Instead he insisted I drive some of his students to San Francisco for a month-long course entitled Arts in the City, May 1971.

"But I need a drama course in order to get a job, Sam."

"Trust me." It was paid travel. Mars came along. Sam made sure we saw a performance of *One Flew Over the Cuckoo's Nest,* a play adapted by Dale Wasserman from Ken Kesey's novel.

When we returned to Iowa, he arranged the promised course for me. Independent Study in Drama. He was the president of the community theater in that town of Waverly, Iowa. I was to single-handedly produce *Cuckoo's Nest.* I started from scratch and learned from books how to build the set, do the sound and lighting, arrange for programs, tickets, costumes, props—the whole asylum.

The play was a success, but it still wouldn't slip me past the closed gates of upper academe. I wished it would have. At least Larry's thought had been kind. He was disappointed, too. However, the want ad right beneath the one Larry had circled read: "Teach English in Japan."

"Mars, want to go to Japan?"

"How soon?"

Some small Iowa towns are extremely conservative *and don't like so much* those people who are different. So I silk-screened a bumper sticker for them: "Charles City. Love it or Leave it."

It was on the back bumper of my car as I drove out of town, with Janis Joplin singing a song in the attic of my mind: *"Freedom's just another word for nothing left to lose."*

......

An Arab fisherman off the coast of East Africa cast a net from his dhow and brought up a brass urn. It was corked with lead that had been stamped when molten with the seal of Solomon. The fisherman excitedly pried open the cork, and in an explosive gust, out came a huge jinni.

"How many wishes am I granted?" asked the fisherman, rubbing his hands in anticipation.

"Only one," answered the jinni.

"In that case, I wish for countless wishes," chuckled the fisherman. He had been ready with that one.

The jinni shook his head. "You did not let me finish. Now that I am free from the urn, the only wish I will grant you is for you to choose the manner of your own death."

The fisherman was shocked. He asked for time to contemplate such a "delicious" choice. Finally he came up with his selection.

"You know, when you came gushing out just now, it almost scared me to death. If I were to get closer to the mouth of the urn, that explosion would surely kill me. It would be an honor to die such a death by your hands. Therefore, I wish for you to go back inside the brass bottle and come out the same way."

The jinni did as he was told.

"Now, to make it seem more real, I'll put the stopper back in."

Pinball Wizard

Living off the
Fat of Japan

Sometimes I find myself
Alone
On the other side of the wall
Free

WE LEFT THE UNITED STATES FOR JAPAN in early April 1976, five years from the date of Mars's accident. Like Midwesterners, the Japanese are conservative and feel very uncomfortable with people who are different. In fact, in Japan the word for "different" is the same as for "wrong." Consensus reality is even stronger in Japan than in Iowa, but I felt at home at once. For the first time in my life, I had an understandable reason for feeling that I was different, an outsider.

In Japan I was constantly seeing things I didn't understand. Some things I guessed right about; some I misinterpreted entirely. A large pile of experiences grew that I allowed myself to perhaps never understand.

Surprisingly, this didn't make my life any more difficult. In many ways it was easier. If I didn't understand, mistakes were understandable, maybe even forgivable. It's OK to make mistakes? This was news to me.

> *Good judgment from your experience comes.*
> *Remember this is how it's always done.*
> *If you do something just for fun*
> *That turns out really dumb,*
> *Experience from your rotten judgment comes.*

Mars and I went for an afternoon stroll through a fashionably sleazy section of Shinjuku, a busy area of Tokyo filled with bars, discos, and short-time love hotels that were mostly closed for the daylight hours. We came across a coffee shop—one of thousands in the area, but this one with a sign saying it was for feminists only: men would be allowed entry only if escorted by a woman. This in male-dominated Japan? Mars insisted we go in. The reception was less than jolly, but we found a table near the door and sat down for a cup.

Through the door pops a petite Japanese woman with very young eyes, though she was slightly past the bloom of her youth: "Hi. My name is Yoneyama Mamako. Maybe you heard of me. I was on TV in the States as a teenager many . . . uh . . . years ago."

She begins miming: taking up needle and thread and sewing her fingers together one at a time, then pulling the thread through and under her elbow and tugging on it to wave good-bye. I remembered seeing this routine on TV when I was a kid and attempting to imitate it.

"Why did you come to Japan? What do you want to learn?" she asked.

I was startled by the question. I hadn't really thought about Japan as anything except that it wasn't Iowa. (My apologies to Iowa. It wasn't about you. It was about egoistic me, way too much.) Tokyo had provided a convenient, entertaining yet irrefutable illusion. Still, I did miss the thrill of the stage, of getting scared to death before I went on and then losing myself by dissolving into a character.

I answered that I wanted to learn about Japanese theater. She agreed to introduce me to someone who could help, although she didn't care for the person because his attitude toward women was so, so . . . Japanese. (She had recently introduced Japan to the concept of marriage by yearly contract. After a year she decided against renewing her contract.) She invited us to come see a Noh play, whatever that was.

To the piercing strains of a Japanese flute, eight ashen-faced old men crawl through the miniature door in the wall at the side of the stage. They face me in two rows, folding their legs beneath their skirts, and begin droning a dirgelike chant that only the gods could love. Classical Noh drama unfolds at the pace pine needles grow. I was bored to tears.

What is going on? Half of the audience is sleeping or nodding. The other half is busily picnicking from their *obento* box lunches. Some are actually concentrating on the play by looking at the book in their hands rather than the stage. The language of Noh is so ancient that even the elderly need these scripts in order to understand the play. Reminds me of pious midwestern church members reading along in their private pocket Bibles while the preacher reads the Epistle for the day. Had kind of the same feeling.

I must have dozed. The crowd stirs as the last Noh actor glides over a bridge extending from the left side of the stage. The curtain descends behind him. Intermission? I join the flow of people moving toward the lobby, but as I reach the aisle, pandemonium breaks out behind me.

Onstage a terrified servant, Taro Kaja, scurries about pursued by his irate master dressed as a fourteenth-century country lord, a daimyo. The mimed actions are broad compared with the staid movements of the previous performance. I can't understand the language but somehow feel the humor; maybe it was merely the contrast.

This, I learned, was another type of Japanese drama, comical Kyōgen. After the performance I was introduced to Mr. Juro Zenchiku, the actor who had played Taro Kaja that day.

At his request I called him, and we made an appointment to meet at the Hachiko statue. Hachiko was a dog famous for his loyalty to his master, who disappeared one day. For many years after, every day at the same time Hachiko waited in vain for his master to return. Right next to the butcher shop, he waited.

Now a statue sits surrounded by a plaza teeming with people who have arranged a meeting. Juro must have seen me first, for he began calling out my name, but he was looking in the other direction. I turned my back on him and called out his name. We began circling the crowd, calling each other's name, spiraling inward until we bumped into each other from behind.

We turned simultaneously. He put his hand out to shake as I bowed. I quickly unbowed and put my hand out as he switched and bowed deeply, his nose bumping my hand. Organic street theater in Tokyo.

Juro took me to his favorite bar, a small second-floor *nomiya* called Okinawa. We went there so often I soon became known there by name, Wayne-san. My outsider status began to slip. With me Juro practiced his English while he introduced me to Japan through the backstage door, behind the facade of what I saw as charade.

Living off the Fat of Japan

I was invited to go cherry-blossom viewing at Ueno Park in northern Tokyo. Traditionally, Japanese would drink tea and create poems to the falling cherry blossoms. The falling ones! Why? The answer was *wabi-sabi*.

Juro tried to translate the concept. It was its transience that made beauty even more beautiful. If something is shown to be impermanent, the last moments of existence have an increased meaning, an added quality of beautiful. *Wabi-sabi*.

Ichigo ichie
One moment
One chance

What? The fact that I am dying increases my beauty? I didn't get it.

Cherry viewing in modern Tokyo has evolved. Now the ground is carpeted with crowded picnic blankets covering every open area of the public park whether there be a cherry tree around or not. Poems are rarely, if ever, written. And the blossoms are usually viewed while the head tilts back to receive yet more sake. Inevitably, I was in need of a restroom.

In those days in Japan, it was common for men to use the sidewalks at night or the bushes during the day. This is not condoned, and yet it is impolite to notice someone being so rude. There is a story of police in hot pursuit of a pickpocket on foot. He turns into a dead-end alley. With no way to escape, he faces the wall as if he is urinating, and the police run right by him. He is culturally invisible. On the day of the cherry-blossom viewing, however, there was no place unoccupied for me to choose this option, and the line, even at the men's john, was too long. I was desperate. I started walking, hurriedly looking for alternatives.

I came across what appeared to be a museum. I was happy to pay the admission. They mistook my haste for excitement.

"You like *shodo?*" The welcome lady at the door spoke in nervous English.

"*Shodo?*" I answered, not knowing what I was saying. I looked up at a whole bunch of large paper scrolls hanging all around the room. Seemed to me someone was using a lot of paper to clean out his or her brush. "I love *shodo,*" I answered.

She asked me to sign the guest book, which I did in the Japanese way. "*Oo-Ay Ee-*n"—I only knew how to write my first name. I felt like a child, and I needed a bathroom now!

"We don't have many foreigner come our museum. We so happy you enjoy, I think. I show you special room. Bery bery best *shodo.*"

No! I think, yet I follow politely, silently, achingly. She escorts me to a room full of even more black brush marks on scrolls. A room full of words I can't read. And no toilet.

Toilet. Toilet. What's the word for toilet! My mind is racing; my eyes are watering; I am crossing my legs.

Living off the Fat of Japan

Benjo. That's it! "Benjo," I blurt out and get the desired result. I learned later that I had used a slang word for something that is worse than an outhouse. The person who told me was too embarrassed to explain.

I felt guilty because I had lied about liking *shodo*. The guide couldn't have been more gracious and didn't seem to notice how crimson my face was. I hadn't yet learned that you can always tell when you are doing something horribly wrong in Japan: nobody is looking. So after I had relieved myself—there has to be a more compelling word for that experience—I felt duty bound to go back and spend time looking at those brush marks.

They did this on purpose? I mean, really? This is the pinnacle of their culture? What's the attraction? I don't get it.

......

For those first six months, Tokyo was Salvador Dalí waltzing a tango with Disney World. It was a giddy time, like the first blush from drinking sake. Speaking of which, in Japan you fill the glass of those around you but never your own. The beverage comes as a blessing from others so that you can say thank you. It took me many years to realize how important this is. I might have caught on sooner considering all the practice I had.

My underage students threw a party, my first in Tokyo, apparently in order to celebrate celebrating. I was invited to be a chaperone and was paid by the school to attend. I had nothing to lose. Paid to party. All right! It was to be held at a rented banquet room on the seventh floor of a building full of discos and karaoke bars in busy Shinjuku.

I get off the train and make my way down the steps from the platform to the correct exit. This is a decisively important first step. Miss this and you will be lost, perhaps forever. I follow the map I have been given as if it were a thread through a labyrinth.

The lights reflect off the lacquered streets, for it has just misted. I just missed it, so I carry my umbrella closed.

Flashing signs are ciphers in unreadable script reflected and distorted by the shining wet pavement. I don't understand the written messages and concentrate on the distortions. It gives me another reason for not understanding an ever-changing world. It makes not understanding more acceptable.

(One night Mars was very late returning to our apartment. It was only a twenty-minute walk from the train station. I was starting to have to pretend not to worry. She came home laughing at herself. It seems she had become so engrossed in the lights reflected in the puddles that she missed her turn and continued in the wrong direction for a couple of miles before realizing what she'd done.)

Lights blaze an Asian Las Vegas of colors and moving scenes, a neon bird flying off into the distance. On

Living off the Fat of Japan

the sidewalk I come close to bumping into a very preg-
nant woman wearing a T-shirt: "YOU ASK FOR IT AND YOU
GOT IT." I probably would have remembered. A carnival
of military music. *Pachinko.* Bells ringing, a scream of
streaming hollow-centered ball bearings.

At the party, platters of sushi, sashimi, cold tem-
pura, rolls of rice, and sake, whiskey *"made in Japan, you
think OK?"* And beer: *"You like Japan beer?"* Glass empty.
"More sake?" "More sashimi?" "More beer?" "What's this
I'm eating?" "More beer?" "Sure." "Restroom?" Return.
My plate full, all cups full, party over, down elevator.
What? Even parties are on a schedule? Rented room.
Time's up. Door opens. And then the evening begins.

A student lies passed out on the floor, her short
skirt hiked up, exposing panties. Fortunately, I am not
the one in charge. An old Tokyo hand, a long-timer who
speaks fluent Japanese, tells some female students to
pull down her skirt for decency's sake and help the girl
however they can. He finds out where she lives and asks
who among us chaperones lives the closest. I do, I discover. But I don't know Tokyo or any of the language.

The old Tokyo pro hands me a bill with "10,000"
written on it and waves at a taxi with two fingers, which
I find out later means we are willing to pay twice the
normal fare.

Another teacher, Melissa, volunteers to ride along
and help me, thank God, so we sandwich the girl in
between us in the backseat of the taxi, and off we go

through the drizzly night. We expected the girl to be able to give the driver her precise address. However, the girl, who in our classroom would not venture a single word in English, now refuses to speak Japanese. It seems she just lost her foreign boyfriend and is heart-broken, a modern Madame Butterfly.

"I love him from the heart of my bottom."

"No," the English teacher in me corrects. "That should be, uh, well? It's not exactly wrong." Clearing throat. "What's your address?"

"Tom. I love you. Tom. Don't leave."

"Your address?"

"Tom, where are you? I need you, Tom. Tom!" She is crying.

"I'm Tom." I say. Mel frowns and rolls her eyes. It's the only thing I could come up with fast. "I'm Tom. Tell me what your address is, Honey, in Japanese for the driver so I can get you home, OK?"

"Tom. Come closer." I do, and she moans. "Oh, Tom. I do not feel well."

Mel: "Do you think you are going to be sick?" The girl nods her head. "What's the word for 'stop' in Japanese?"

"'Stop'? Uh, I don't know."

The driver hears me. *"Stoppu? Stoppu?"* He assesses the situation in his rearview mirror, swings the taxi over to the curb through several lanes of busy traffic, and comes to a full stop next to the curb. Mel jumps out and in so doing spills her purse into the gutter flowing with

Living off the Fat of Japan

rainwater. The girl leans over. Mel frantically tries to collect her drenched things and get them back into her purse before they're swept into the storm sewer and also before the remains of the night's party arrive. I run around the car one way, the taxi driver the other way. He is relieved that his taxi has stayed clean. I'm watching the Fellini movie I am living.

Meanwhile, a man and his dog that were out for a walk had stopped to relieve themselves. When the taxi door flew open both were in midstream, the dog with its leg in the air. The streams stopped immediately. I shouldn't have noticed, but I'm not Japanese.

The girl finally yields her address. Up the elevator holding her up, hallway, metal door. Mel presses the door button. Mom answers, looks at her daughter relieved.

Daughter steps out of our grasp—"Hi, Mom"—and withers to the ground. Mom looks at daughter, then up at Mel, and finally at me. A smorgasbord of fear, embarrassment, confusion, and anger is served on her face.

I know so little Japanese, but still I could have done better than *"Arigato."* I should have said, *"Gomen nasai"*— "Please take no offense." But not me. I come up with a stupid "thank-you" at the wrong time.

......

The first six months were so full, I forgot at times that I was dying. Not so New Year's Eve, 1977, on vacation in the Philippines. Mars had taken off on a trip to have a lunch of chicken-foot soup with some village women of a family we had just met. I wasn't invited along. Genders in those cultures don't often mix socially.

I sat alone at night on quiet Matabunkai Bay, my death fully on my mind. OK, I was having a great time partying, but it meant nothing. Life had turned into a slapstick farce, into theater of the absurd, a very sick joke.

I gaze out into the waves invisible in the darkness until they break, leaving a line of phosphorescent green-blue lightning. Another wave of water energy sparks millions of these little animals to flash out of existence.

Is that it? Is that the sole purpose of their brief life: to be agitated so that they outline a wave for me to see. What if no one saw them? Would it make a difference? Probably not. What if I weren't here? Would it make a difference? Why would it?

There it is in a nut's cell. I'm afraid I don't have long to live in this flip-of-the-coin life of mine. It all seems so meaningless, I can't even cry. No use feeling sorry for myself. Everyone dies. Lots of people live meaningless lives. They live to work to live to work. For what? Got enough to eat already. Got more things than fit in the house. Is it whoever dies with the most toys wins? It isn't that I'm any more important than anyone else. It's that everyone else's life looks to be as unimportant as mine.

But I'm still alive. At least I can fill the time I have left if not with meaning at least with intent. I say out loud, the stars my witness: *"From now on I'll do whatever I want to do—as much as I can get away with."*

"So what do you want to do?" Who said that? I become conscious of my junior-high teacher, Mrs. Geronami, standing next to me on the beach, her hair tied back severely, her hands planted heavily on her hips.

"I would like to be a writer. But what are the chances with my luck? I suppose the coin could land on its edge. Fat chance that."

"A writer? That surprises me. I always thought you would go into math. However, *if you want to be a writer you have to write.*" She taps her finger on her hip. *"Well? What are you waiting for?"*

"Get serious. Look at this place. Smell the air. Look at those waves. This is better than a postcard. And I am supposed to go back to my stuffy little room and start writing? Now? This minute? You are out of your mind," I sassed. "I'll start tomorrow."

"I thought you said you wanted to be a writer."

She's right. I have vowed to do what I want. If I want to be a writer, I have no excuse for not writing. Starting now.

So I return to my sauna of a room made of concrete blocks that hold the heat of yesterday until sunrise, and beneath a five-watt lightbulb hanging by its own wire I sit staring at the empty paper. I have no idea what to write about.

Stars When the Sun Shines

At that time I couldn't face my fear, my cancer, my anger. I certainly couldn't make sense out of my life in Tokyo. After thinking for a long time in vain . . .

An ant crawls onto the page. "My pen is following an ant across the paper."

"Profound. Put that one on your gravestone, Wayne," I thought out loud.

Tokyo Cowboy

WE WERE WORKING FOR THE RIP-OFF Foreign Language University of Kanda, or FLUK. In the advertisement brochure for the school, all the foreigners' eyes were touched up to be sky blue, like Ascended Masters. At opening invocation we were first introduced to our students by the school founder, Mr. Sano. He admonished them in Japanese to be tolerant of the foreigners even if we smelled bad. It wasn't because we were unclean, he explained. It was because we ate so much meat.

The year went downhill from there. When one of our fellow teachers, a close friend, flipped out, the school tried to deny responsibility for his hospitalization in the psych ward and his flight home. They finally did pay for his ticket and the accompanying doctors and the straitjacket, medications, etc.

My friend had been going off his rocker for a while. It was obvious. He would go into a crowded *pachinko* parlor only to sneak out the back door to ditch his tail. He started talking about how the fluorescent lights flickered because they contained a camera that filmed us in the interval. His paranoia was huge. I didn't believe him about the cameras, but I understood where he was coming from. For me, his cameras were a metaphor for how I always felt that Big Brother was watching me in Tokyo. Eventually, I started picking up telepathic messages from him. *What is going on?*

After eleven months in Tokyo working for FLUK, old man Sano transformed himself into an ancestor tablet. We teachers were docked pay if we didn't wait in line at Sano's funeral so that photos could be taken for promotional purposes. Mars and I stayed home.

A fellow teacher, Jan, who was, incidentally, my Charles City friend Larry's sister-in-law—small world—came over to our tiny apartment to ask me to talk some sense into her. It seems a crazy Japanese man was looking for real blue-eyed foreigners who wanted to come with him and join a rodeo as cowboys and cowgirls. What should she do? She was as angry with the school as I was. And she missed riding. I told her that even though I had never ridden a horse, I'd join up with her in an instant if I weren't married.

"I'll start packing. I'm coming along," said Mars.

We flew to Okinawa and joined the American Buffalo Wild West Rodeo Traveling Caravan Show. Logically, since American sports such as baseball, bowling, and golf had transferred to Japan so effortlessly, a rodeo show would be a sure thing. What could be more American than a rodeo? Tsuruda, a round-headed man with a bowling-ball haircut and a missing pinkie, was able to convince some backers to invest in such a venture.

The first day in Okinawa, we went shopping for tailor-made gaudy western shirts in turquoise, magenta, pink, and yellow, with flowery western-cut shoulders in clashing contrast. We were fitted for a custom-made pair of white cowboy boots; mine came with a nail in the toe of the left boot. A cowboy hat was a must, of course, and, at that same leather shop, a green suede jacket with fringe along the arms and back.

"There weren't no horses when we got to Okinawa," Marv, the rodeo foreman, informed us. They were being shipped from Hokkaido, and arrived seasick. Meanwhile, we practiced roping posts by day. That was fun. I had a feel for the motion, loved the way my body countered the centrifugal force naturally.

We all lived at a hotel except for the "Indians," who were to be played by Japanese. They had to sleep in a teepee and cook on an open fire. They were a little bitter on cold, rainy nights, and we never bonded with them. It was amazing how we were able to re-create

Tokyo Cowboy

conditions of ethnic isolation so similar to those of the American West.

I gave myself the assignment of writing at least two hundred words a day. Since we weren't doing anything different from day to day, that assignment became nearly impossible. And I wanted to be a writer?

The first show was a fiasco. Nothing went right except for the exceptionally talented trick rider, who left the next day when he didn't get paid. The calf roping was called because the small, underage calf found a way to squeeze through the fence we'd built. A real cowboy from the military base chased the calf down two city blocks and carried it back to the arena on his shoulders.

When the Conestoga wagon covered with brown butcher paper that had been soaked with kerosene was pulled out into the center of the arena, it looked kind of impressive in a homemade sort of way. When they coaxed children out of the crowd and gave each a feathered headdress and a bow and arrow and had them form a circle around the wagon, it was kind of cute. Giving them flaming arrows wasn't the best idea, because those few arrows that did hit the paper went right through toward the kids on the other side. Madness. And the paper didn't catch fire. The kerosene had evaporated.

One of the "Indians" crept out and crawled into the back of the wagon. He tried to light the fire with his Zippo. Couldn't in that wind.

In desperation the boss mounted the camel—camel? don't ask—and shot out, or rather trotted out, of the chute. The strap hadn't been properly secured; it fell loose and was dragging in the dirt. The camel would not buck despite Tsuruda's spurs. It stuck out its green tongue at the crowd. The same "Zippo Indian" crawled out again and tightened the strap right across the camel's testicles. Ouch!

The camel shot straight up in the air, launching the unsuspecting boss like an early NASA rocket forming a perfect arc to the ground. Bonk! Boss was spread out like the pentagonal man and starry-eyed.

He regains consciousness. We help him stand. He pushes us away. "Leave me alone! I am OK! I can take care of myself!" he barks in Japanese. He takes one step and falls flat on his nose. Ouch!

The next day, roping practice was dreary. It didn't help that the boss came out with a Band-Aid on his nose and caressing his remaining pinkie. He blamed us for yesterday's debacle. We were a sorry, worthless bunch of *gaijin*—the word for "foreigner" always seemed to be used with a touch of scorn. He would teach us how to be cowboys. He'd start with the rope.

He tried to sneak up from behind and rope a cowgirl—who incidentally came from Palm Springs. That rope can hurt if it hits a tender face. Fortunately, she caught a glimpse of him out of the corner of her eye and ran away. He chose a new target and tossed. He wasn't coming close.

If someone else's pain isn't a concern of his, his isn't a concern of mine. I let my lasso fly fifteen feet through

Tokyo Cowboy

air, hover above him for what seems like forever before coming down around him. He begins to run. The rope is at his knees when I jerk it. He falls gracefully. Gee. I didn't know I could do that.

The "cowpokes" sitting on the fence called thumbsdown for me to tie him up like a calf, which I did as a joke. Yesterday's fiasco was forgotten. I let him go right away. It was only a joke, after all. Everyone had a good laugh, but the boss's ended sooner than the rest of ours.

After the usual evening beer-laced feast in the hotel, Marv, the rodeo foreman, walked me back to my room. At the door he said, "You do know that the boss is *yakuza*."

"What's that?"

"The Japanese mafia."

......

The next morning, we flew back to Tokyo. We had no money. Fortunately, a friend bought the TV we had inherited with our apartment for about fifty dollars. I don't know what we would have done if we hadn't had our TV. We had two weeks left on our visa. We needed to find a job and get a sponsor or we would be kicked out of Japan.

We ate samples at various department stores, alternating as much as possible so we wouldn't be recognized as recidi-visitors. (That's a word I just made up, a combination of *recidivist* and *visitor*. They frowned on flagrant repeaters.) Sweets, pickled radish, tasteless cheese, fried whatever, green tea ice cream, brandy. Meanwhile, we looked for work.

Jobs were hard to find. One day I was walking past Sophia University, a highly prestigious institute run by venerable German Jesuits. I paused at the gatehouse, thinking that it probably was a waste of time. I wasn't even Catholic. You just don't walk into a university, especially one such as this, and get a job.

"What was your previous position, Mr. Stier?" How was I going to answer that question? I didn't feel comfortable telling a lie. It would be too confusing. And I blushed too easily.

I was about to leave when the guard asked me what it was that I wanted. I told him I was looking for a job teaching English. It so happened that Father Hancock was just then starting a community college, an adult night school. He was hiring. I was given the job.

When Mars returned to our apartment, she was in tears. The only job she could find meant a great deal of commuting in crowded trains, working nights, and teaching office workers at their place of business under fluorescent lights. Dreary.

The phone rang. Father Hancock. "Wayne, do you happen to know of any other good, qualified English teachers?"

Mars has her teacher's certificate. "Is it OK if we're married?"

"Is she any good?"

Tokyo Cowboy

"She's better than me." Mars also became a professor. Score.

I didn't realize it at the time, but all my wishes were in the process of being answered. First I asked to get out of Iowa, and it was done almost immediately. Then I vowed to do what I wanted even if it meant an obviously bad career move like joining the American Buffalo Wild West Rodeo Traveling Caravan Show. This resulted in a professorship at a prestigious university, like the position I had once coveted but felt I had been barred from.

Writing? I didn't think much about it.

I called Juro after I was given the job at Sophia, and he invited me out for the night to celebrate. I came to him wearing the fringed suede jacket. He appeared outside his gate in a black and gray *haori* cape with pom-pom buttons in the front. It was spontaneous: we traded jackets, mine drowning him like a long cape. I played the night as a traditional Japanese, and he played an American cowboy. Street theater in a cultural mirror.

One time we performed a mock sumo battle in the middle of a busy train station, gathering a cheering, laughing crowd around us. I was so much bigger and a foreigner as well; it became essential that I lose. One time late into the night we played imaginary slow-motion tennis on the train platform over waiting passengers' heads. The game was interrupted when our train pulled in.

Stars When the Sun Shines

Life was good. We worked only four nights a week and only four hours each night, about twenty-eight weeks a year. In class the Japanese are slow to laugh and slow to understand English. They laugh mostly when they get nervous. So I would pretend to be nervous, and they would feel nervous for me and laugh. I did an imitation of Dick Van Dyke's "put on a happy face": Smiling. Wiping my smile away. Putting it back with my hand.

I could see everyone melting into their desks, becoming students and giving themselves an excuse to once again not be able to learn the difficult language of English. I told everyone to stand up. They did. Sit down. They did. I looked disappointed. Stand up again. They did. Sit down. Stand up. Sit down.

"How long do we have to do this?"

"Until someone asks this question. Thank this brave person. If it hadn't been for him speaking English, this classroom may have become a gymnasium."

Beautiful young women would sit unconscious of their uncrossed legs in the front of the class and smile. One of them said after class one day, "I was very interesting during class today."

"Yes, you were," I responded. "But I think you meant 'interested.'"

We played. One student told me that she wasn't sure if she learned any English, but she had so much fun she signed up for the same class again. Eleven times. After the fifth time, I started feeding her the punch lines.

Tokyo Cowboy

To my surprise, the students often applauded when I left the room at the end of class. The first time it happened, I asked another teacher why the Japanese did this. He told me he had never heard of anyone receiving applause.

Between classes one day I decided to attend a lecture given by an Indian philosopher who had developed such a high state of awareness that he was able to talk apparently without ever stopping. He had lectured beyond the two hours I had free between classes. I made my way quietly to the back of the auditorium. As I reached the door, the Indian said directly to me, "Sir. I see you have a watch, but no time. Me, I have no watch, and I have all the time in the world."

I was living inside a machine called Tokyo. Everyone was on time. The trains were on time; during rush hour, some train lines came into the station every ninety seconds. Everyone was busy, hurrying. People would pretend to run across a room. It was proper etiquette in front of one's superior.

......

I read a short story by Abe Kobo. A man comes home drunk at night as usual to his apartment building, one of forty or so identical buildings in his complex. He gets in the elevator and presses the wrong button. He goes down the hall to what he thinks is his home. He walks in. Wife is in the kitchen as usual. They give each other the customary greetings. He sits down in his chair as usual. Something's wrong. The pictures of the kids. We don't have kids. He realizes his mistake and, too embarrassed to say anything, sneaks out and finds his way home.

He becomes tortured that his life is not his. He wants to know that he exists as a separate entity, not just a replaceable part. He decides to contact the *yakuza* and manages to buy a couple of sticks of dynamite—not to use them, but to have them to use. He puts them in his briefcase and gets on his commuter train as scheduled, content in the knowledge that he is now different. He opens up his morning newspaper: "Man arrested in subway for carrying dynamite."

A packed train passes as I wait on my bicycle, a necktie sticking out between the doors and flying in the wind. The "salary man" must have made a desperate backward dive through the closing traincar doors. Those doors close hard and hurt, yet every train sees someone taking the chance.

I asked my students why they do it. Does their boss dock them ninety seconds of pay if they are late? Or when they return home drunk and late at night, which is normal in Tokyo, is their wife standing hands on hips at the door demanding an explanation: "And what mischief have you been up to for the past minute and a half?"

Tokyo Cowboy

Time Savings Bank

They've stolen all the time that we have saved
And hid it in a time vault, like a grave.
We're going to need a very clever sleuth
To discover and uncover the whole truth.
What becomes of all those precious seconds?
Are they hidden in a vault and then forgotten?

We saved up so much time in drive-thru lines,
And scarfing food while driving saves more time,
And then we speed although it is a crime
Just so that we arrive and just in time.
Where are all those seconds that we shaved?
Where are all those minutes that we saved?

We're living twice as much on double time
Without a reason and without a rhyme
In muddled and befuddled time engulfed.
Where is the bank that keeps the hidden vault?
My account for saving time is in default.

Up to the teller I will firmly walk
And state: "I wish to make a full withdrawal
Of all my extra hours laid away,
And spend them smelling flowers all the day."
I'll open up my Savings Time Account
And withdraw the whole entire full amount

All that the Savings Bankers will allow
I'll spend it all with interest
With interest on now.

That evening after work I went to my favorite *nomiya,*
watering hole-in-the-wall. At the end of the evening I
took off my watch, strapped it over a beer bottle, and
left. I was going off time. The proprietor friend tried to
return the watch to me on my next visit, but I refused.

......

Juro had decided to be my host to the real Japan, the
traditional Japan. His English was improving, and he
was enjoying my world of illusion. He gave me compli-
mentary tickets to the Noh theater any time I wished to
attend. I did a few times.

We went to the Japanese version of *Othello,* which
they pronounced "Osello." I remember vividly the lead
actor prancing across the stage crying in Japanese about
the errant handkerchief: *"Hanka chee. Hanka chee."* I felt
Shakespeare had lost something in the translation. Des-
demona was played by a beautiful young woman with an
Adam's apple.

After the performance we went backstage, where I
met the *onnagata,* a male actress, the now-famous Tamas-
aburō. He even drank his tea as a woman, his movements
so refined that actresses couldn't compete with his femi-
ninity onstage. His actions were quintessentially feminine. Elegant. I never did my Richard bit again.

Tokyo Cowboy

One time Juro gave me a ticket to Kabuki theater. Kabuki is more like a revue than a play. Each venue has a combination of best-known and beloved parts of plays that the audience could recite by heart if they wished. The actors are judged as to how well they imitate the revered actors who came before them. It would be like seeing the best of Shakespeare selected from many different plays and splashed together on the same program, with all the actors imitating Laurence Olivier.

I arrived late at the theater, reaching my seat in the middle of a full row of knees just as the first act closed. I hadn't eaten much all day and had only a little money left after allowing for my ticket for the train ride home, so I searched for some cheap food in the lobby. Much of what was available at my price range may not have been edible for all I knew and was not worth the gamble. I found something that looked like an ice-cream sandwich, which I shouldn't have eaten.

The next section of Kabuki began shortly after I returned to my seat. Onstage a couple of servants or perhaps family members were crying. The audience began to cry, too. More crying, building in intensity. Enter samurai dude in purple with white under-kimono. Crying crescendos. Not him, but everyone else onstage. Everyone around me. He tells them to leave. He prefers to be alone. The other actors leave the stage crying.

He kneels and slowly pulls out his sword, wrapping it with white cloth. He removes his outer purple kimono and is now dressed only in the white under-kimono, the color of death in Japan. Tears gushing everywhere around me. Some women in the audience are already on their third *hanka chee*. As he ceremoniously places the tip of the sword tight against his abdomen, mine decides to loudly sing the ice-cream sandwich song. *Gomen nasai*. People struggled not to notice.

......

The second summer in Japan, I decided to visit the United States to attend my folks' fortieth wedding anniversary. When I told Juro, he sighed. His one dream in life was to have the opportunity to go to America. It was all but impossible for a Noh actor to do so. Before the family of actors he belonged to would allow him the freedom to take such a journey, he had to be invited to perform. It was next to impossible to get that permission.

He had been generous to me for a long time and refused any attempt I made to pay him back. Because of my present employment, I could afford his plane ticket and could supply food and lodging for the trip. I could even arrange for some venues for performances. It occurred to me that with the exception of asking Mars to be my wife, I had never been offered the opportunity to make someone else's lifelong dream come true. So on a whim I invited him to come along.

Juro performed in my hometown, in the St. John's Lutheran Church basement, to the utter bemusement of my relatives, who had already thought me eccentric.

Tokyo Cowboy

Putting on the Zen

ONE DAY SOON AFTER WE HAD RETURNED from our trip to the States, Juro suggested, "If you wish to know Japan, you must study her ancient art."

"Which one?" I baited him.

"It doesn't matter. Whichever one you are interesting in." He paused. "You should study Kyōgen, I think."

It seems the tables had been turned. My generosity was merely a repayment for his, which had been offered initially so that he could have a private language teacher while he played. Now I had put a burden on Juro's family that they could repay only one way. I needed to become a student of Noh drama. It was a type of theater

I found boring. The plays were written by a guy named Zeami about the time of Charlemagne in an old and obscure dialect that modern Japanese cannot understand. What possible relevance could such esoteric, arcane study have for me in today's world? Yet, it was a gift I could not possibly refuse. I had asked to be onstage in Japan. I couldn't reject an answer to my request. You take the ride that's offered.

My friend Juro became Zenchiku-sensei, my teacher. Or rather, my *honored* teacher, because *sensei* connotes so much more respect than does the word *teacher*. And I became his *deshi,* meaning "disciple," rather than student. Actually, I became an *uchi deshi,* or house student. Often when a troupe was in need of extra actors or when a son was incompetent, they would adopt one of the more promising servants of the house.

At the first lesson, Zenchiku-sensei met me at the door of his home, made certain I removed my shoes in the *genkan,* the entryway, and directed me to wait for him in the studio upstairs. For a Japanese home, his upstairs was an unheard-of luxury of open space. A shining wooden stage, although not the size of an actual theater, occupied three-fourths of the room. The decor was studied simplicity: a scroll painting of cherry blossoms on the wall, a vase with cherry blossoms on a low table. A few fallen petals. Two flat pillows lay on the tatami floor beside a short-legged table. I waited to be told which pillow would be mine.

Zenchiku-sensei arrived with a pot of bitter green tea and two cups without handles. He used neither of the pillows. Noh actors never will, on or off stage. He served me individually wrapped sweets to balance the flavor of the tea. By the time we had finished the tea, I had a pile of crumpled wrappers in front of me. He, on the other hand, had only one piece of paper, which he had folded into a neatly knotted rectangle and placed back on the table. Lesson number one.

"What do you think is Kyōgen?" he asked me.

"Comic Noh?" I guessed incorrectly.

"If you go to a Kyōgen performance expecting to see only comedy," he informed me, "you may be disappointed, even shocked by apparent cruelty."

This is because not all Kyōgen plays are intended to be humorous. Rather, they depict the drama of everyday life in fourteenth-century Japan. Kyōgen began during the Muromachi period (1380–1466), about the same time Noh drama took form. Kyōgen and Noh always have been separate disciplines, yet their histories are intertwined. Often a Kyōgen actor will appear as a servant or commoner in a Noh play, but no lofty Noh actor would ever deign to appear professionally in a Kyōgen play. In a way Kyōgen is the mirror of Noh. A Noh actor must always use his right leg to step out of his gate. The Kyōgen actor must always use his left foot first.

Noh is poetic. It is a stylized dance-drama dedicated to the gods. Kyōgen, on the other hand, is about us. It is the mirror that shows a smudge of grease on our nose.

"Kyōgen is about people who are too much carried away in their sentiments," sensei explained while I squirmed uncomfortably on my knees on the floor. *Too much in my sentiments, am I? Easy for him to say. He thinks he has a long life to live. I know I don't. This is real slow.*

The two written characters that make up the word Kyōgen can be read variously as either "totally involved in talk" or "crazy speak." I can relate.

"To know Kyōgen," sensei continued, "you will learn how people lived six centuries ago. You must study all of Japan's ancient art: dance, ikebana or flower arrangement, martial art, the tea ceremony, *shodo*—so that you can do them in mime. Do you know about *shodo*?"

"Very little," I answered truthfully, blushing from the memory of that cherry-blossom party.

He placed a plain white sheet of rice paper on the table and, with water poured from a small ceramic vessel, began to prepare ink from a solid black block.

Once the ink had been rubbed to the proper thickness, he turned and faced the paper and breathed. First he wrote in Japanese script. Then he used the same brush to copy it in the letters of the alphabet for my benefit. He put each stroke on the paper precisely, like a painter, always in relation to the way he breathed. Yet on the very last line he made a mistake; it was not erasable.

......

I was invited over to the apartment of a young, dark-eyed Javanese beauty, so I took my wife with me. The room was perfumed with the exotic aromas of coconut, kafir lime, and clove. We reminisced with her about the magic of life in Java.

She excused herself, using her hand as a knife to cut out of the bubble of our conversation without doing damage. She returned carrying a sarong full of countless little white dots on an indigo field. She had painted the dots herself, she said proudly. She searched for something and found it. One dot was a quarter inch long. "That's where I fell asleep," she giggled, fully forgiven by herself. "Don't you see? That is the art."

......

I felt sorry for sensei for botching it after all the trouble he took, but he didn't seem to mind. He finished the rest of the line with the same calm care.

After the ink had dried, he knelt formally and instructed me to do the same. He chanted the poem twice. Then he taught me how to bow in humble appreciation—which one could do without the least bit of humility because it was required to be done in a precise manner—and the lesson was over.

I heard that same chant numerous times at every lesson for countless weekly lessons thereafter. Each time, I was to repeat it after sensei, and he would meticulously correct my pronunciation, my rhythm, my breathing.

Although he was only two-thirds my size, I strained to produce half his volume.

"Like most native American speaker, you have beautiful voice because you have thousands of sounds in your language. Japanese have only one hundred and ten sounds. But you cannot use natural human voice, I think." Then he chanted the piece once more, and I watched the blood vessels bulge dangerously in his forehead. This was natural?

"You probably don't need a microphone onstage." I said, a master of the obvious.

"Yes, we don't. We already have," he informed me. In the vacant area beneath every Noh stage hang large empty clay pots aiming in various directions. They amplify the sound on the stage above. And white rocks around the stage reflect sunlight for outside theaters.

"Like footlights," I said, beginning to understand the ingenuity of ancient Japanese stagecraft.

We chanted again and again week after week. I found a way to add to my volume. I channeled the pain from my cramping feet burdened by my buttocks and smashed into the hard wooden floor. I channeled that pain loudly into my voice.

With concentration I tried to mimic every nuance, pitch, and breath. Often in doing so I felt as if I were mocking the Japanese. Juro didn't seem offended.

Sensei used his closed paper fan to tap out a rhythm that was always different from the one I was chanting.

The rhythm was foreign to me, elusive, as inconsistent as a path in a Japanese garden—that is, until I finally understood the pattern and the gardens.

One day a simple yet perfectly constructed wooden box rested on the low table. After we had bowed our ritual hello in timed sequence and precise order, he ceremoniously opened the box and took out something wrapped in an elegant cloth. With studied care he placed it in front of me on the low table and opened the cloth one side at a time to reveal an unpainted but highly polished carved wooden mask with thin slits beneath each eye. The workmanship was masterful. This mask had been passed down in his family through countless generations to his father through his grandfather, who had been a Living National Treasure.

A Living National Treasure! What would that be like?

"When I put on mask my face cannot explain anything. I cannot use my mouth or my eye to show emotion. Notice when I put on mask and keep eyes straight, the mask is looking up. In order for the mask to be looking straight, my head has to be angled down. The difference is slight, if you get my means."

He told me that the slightest movement of the mask has subtle but profound meaning. *The change of only a few degrees in the angle of the mask will mean the difference between light reflecting joy or the shadows of extreme sadness.*

"So actor cannot move his head. He must keep at precise correct angle at all time. Good actor get near edge of stage. Bad actor fall off."

I asked if I could hold the mask. "No!" he answered with uncharacteristic abruptness. The Japanese usually avoid saying a direct no. "Noh and Kyōgen are living museums. This part of museum is traditional charge of my family. Only professional actor with permission of family may wear mask."

At another practice session I had to wait for a student to finish. When he did, he bowed his appreciation and handed sensei an envelope. Sensei explained that it was a customary gift of money, a thank-you for the honor of being a student. So how much was the normal thank-you? "I am artist, not a merchant."

At the next session, sensei told me of a play in New York where a Noh actor and an American performed together in Japanese costumes. Each night after the performance the American's costume had to be drycleaned because he perspired so much. The Japanese costume was merely hung up on a pole.

Appearing to change the subject, he asked, "Have you noticed my *tabi?*" He showed me his heavy-soled stocking-slippers with a slit like a mitten that separates the big toe from the rest. He wondered if I would like to wear *tabi*.

"Not particularly," I answered honestly. Then he told me to look at the shine on the polished stage floor. After every one of my lessons he had to mop the floor to erase my footprints.

I found *tabi* large enough for my feet in a section of a department store with clothes for sumo wrestlers. After the next lesson he told me it was time I learned to dance.

"Dance? I thought I was going to learn acting," I whined.

"You must first know how to move onstage," he answered.

It wasn't all that easy. I had to rise from my knees, broomstick-on-the-backbone straight, and stand and move on numb feet.

"In Noh and Kyōgen the body should form a straight line as if a thread pulled the actor from the top of his head, a straight line drawn through man between heaven and earth. There is no empty feeling, no place where my power goes out. All the power is kept inside. It is same in Japanese martial arts. The enemy has no way of attacking me when I stand in this way."

It felt as though the arms, legs—the whole body— were being controlled by many invisible strings, and I was the puppet. Philosophically I learned that Noh wishes to reduce the number of physical explanations made by the body. Ideally it wishes for zero motion. In reality it limits the motions to the very least necessary to convey the essential idea.

The eyes remain constantly focused one meter in front of the actor. They do not change—eyes frozen in front even as the head turns. There is no show of expression. No acting.

Putting on the Zen

"The actor is a dot pointing out the empty stage." What does that mean? "Life on this plane is illusion. Illusion on the stage points to itself and to the illusion in all life." What does that mean?

He continued: "You might say Noh acting is to movie acting as a line drawing is to an oil painting."

Those who don't understand this stage convention, this Zen philosophy of limited movement, have said, "A Noh play is no play." They are wrong. This limitation of form is basic not only to Noh but also to most Japanese traditions—from flower arrangement to the tea ceremony, and, yes, to *shodo*.

Oh!

Every movement on the polished wooden stage was to be done in complete balance, the center of gravity slightly forward, with the weight on the toes. These movements were often so slow that balance was difficult. *I had no idea how much I had been relying on velocity for my equilibrium.*

In moving, the foot is slid along the stage, the toe lifted at the last moment. "The reason for this rests in history of Japanese. We are nature-loving people. We want to keep touch with spirit of earth, so we maintain contact with earth as long as possible by walking this way."

"Same way a farmer would walk in a slippery rice paddy, wouldn't you think?" I suggested, to sensei's dismay.

He taught me to bend my knees slightly when I walked, to turn on stylized pivots, to move with dramatic tension by increasing my speed as I walked, only to stop abruptly.

"Move as if you can trap air between your body and the point where you stop," he coached. The first time I tried this, I slid into the corner post.

At each practice, before I was allowed onto the stage I had to have a closed paper fan stuck into my belt. It was to be positioned precisely on the floor in front of me while I chanted. It was to be opened exactly perpendicular to my eyes, like an extension of my nose, when I danced. The fingers were to be manipulated in such a way that the fan would spin into a new position precisely.

On my first attempt I dropped my fan. Sensei struck my hand hard with his closed fan to show his displeasure. I stopped. I stared at him intensely, controlling my anger. I will not be struck by any man. He glared back with equal intensity, yet I think he understood where I was coming from. That was the last time he ever struck me. That also was the last time I ever dropped my fan.

The fan will be many things in the hands of a Kyō-gen actor. It can be used in mime as a cup of sake from which a character drinks himself royally drunk. It can be drawn from the belt like a samurai's sword or extended from the end of the arm as a fishing pole. The fan can be the moon coming over the mountain and, with a sleight-of-hand movement, the moon's reflection in a sylvan lake.

One day before I went on the practice stage sensei presented me with a plain beige fan, a scraggly pine tree

Putting on the Zen

sketched in black ink on its surface. "The pine tree is symbol for longevity," he told me. "It is also symbol for Noh and Kyōgen. That is why pine tree is always painted on back wall of every stage or growing beside outside stage. In the beginning actors were employed to perform by the shrines, most specifically Kasuga Shrine in Nara, where Japanese drama began. They were to perform before pine tree to honor the gods. So pine tree means gods' presence."

Pointing to the fan, he said, "This type of fan belongs only to Ohkura-*ryu,* the Ohkura school of Kyōgen."

I learned that each segment of a Noh performance is the province of a particular school, or *ryu.* The flute performers are one specialty group; there are four schools for flute. Many more schools exist for each of the three types of drums. There are two for Kyōgen, supplying the secondary actors of a Noh play, and several schools for the primary Noh actors. Each school differs slightly on how things are done. One does not switch schools.

No one can perform in any area other than the one designated for his group. In other words, a Noh performance is a cooperative effort of many specialists who probably have never practiced together as a unit for that play.

In order to do this, every performer must know how to do all other parts. For instance, a Kyōgen performer must know every part in all 180 Kyōgen plays plus all parts in all the Noh plays in which he might perform. In addition he must have a working knowledge of how to play all the instruments.

"So you see, every play performance is for one and only one time. It will never be the same again. The same performers may never gather together for this play. Even though the play will be performed again, it can never be the same again."

I didn't see it that way. To me everyone in this kind of theater, in this kind of world, was a cog in a machine, a cog that could be immediately replaced if necessary at any moment. It was like the theater was representing the robot mentality of modern Japan. What would be the fun in this kind of theater for me, or for anyone, as an actor? Wouldn't it naturally create mechanical performances?

Of the two schools of Kyōgen—Izumi and Ohkura— the latter is the older, and the former a young splinter whippersnapper that began a mere two hundred years ago. The new school allowed changes in the plays and added new ones to the repertoire. Not so Ohkura. The Zenchiku family can trace itself back to near the origins of Kyōgen. Juro Zenchiku was a nephew of the twenty-fourth-generation head of the school. This school was an unblemished view into the soul of ancient Japan.

He closed the fan and handed it to me. "Now you are truly Ohkura *deshi*." I opened the fan properly, perpendicularly in front of my nose, and looked again at the painted pine. This time it was a work of art.

Putting on the Zen

The fan represented my sleeve in the dance called *Yukiyama,* "Snow Mountain." The emperor is out picking new grass on New Year's Day—they started their year in spring back then—when a late winter snow begins to fall. Instead of brushing the snow off, he carries it on his sleeve and lets it fall on the ground at a chosen spot center stage. His courtiers do the same. They are making a poem out of the event of snow falling. The process is repeated so many times that a small mountain of snow is formed. Oh my! What joy!

Wayne. Wait. Patience.

Snow, I was told, represented good fortune. For one who had grown up in cold Minnesota, it was difficult to understand how anyone could be happy when snow falls on spring grass. To me snow was a strange thing to dance about. It was an even stranger kind of New Year's party.

When I had created what I considered enough snow mountains, when that one dance had become as old to me as winter, I asked, "Don't you think it is time we move on to something new?"

"Do you think you are ready?"

"It is not for me to decide," I answered humbly, as was proper. "But I'm ready," I added truthfully. (In Japan truth is often discounted for the sake of social lubrication. It took me a long time to learn this. For instance, when someone says yes, it does not mean agreement; it merely means they are listening.)

Stars When the Sun Shines

"Very good. Next lesson, new dance."

"Has a foreigner ever performed a Kyōgen play?" I hinted.

"There are many ways to get to top of mountain. We study sometime twenty year before we are ready to perform. You are in hurry. So then I promise you this: within this year you will be on Noh stage in front of audience. But first you must learn more dance."

I had been studying for about a year when I was invited to attend a special practice at Katsuga Shinto shrine in Nara, the very shrine where Noh theater originated seven centuries ago. My parents, who were visiting me at the time, were invited to attend as well. It was important to sensei that we all be there. His family was so excited about the event that they bought me a formal kimono, tailor-made to fit my unusual six-foot height.

During that "rehearsal" I was asked to chant in unison with the head of Ohkura, a low, growl-like tone shooting into my gut. I didn't realize it then, but I am almost certain now that I was adopted that night so that I could rightfully appear on the sacred Noh stage.

The play chosen for me was *Shibiri,* or "Inherited Cramp," an appropriate selection because of the difficulty I had bending my knees enough to sit on my ankles. Briefly, the plot centers on a lazy servant, Taro Kaja, who was to be played by me. He is told to go to town to fetch some fish.

Putting on the Zen

"*Sore wa ikana koto de gozaimasu.* This is a fine kettle of fish. Mind you, I do like fish, but I could lose my taste for it if I have to go down and fetch some every time we want to eat it."

Instead, the servant pretends that he has a sore leg —to be precise, a sore left leg—and is unfortunately unable to do what he so much wishes he could do to please his master. He is so phony, it is syrup.

"*Itayano! Itayano!*"—Ouch! Ouch!—cries Taro Kaja in fake agony.

The master isn't fooled. As a ruse, he pretends to hear his neighbor inviting him to a party.

"What? You plan to have all that delicious party food, oh, and drinks, too?" Taro Kaja is interested. "You want me to bring that clever servant of mine, Taro Kaja? Yes indeed. He is always so much fun to have around at a party, but I am sorry he cannot come today. Unfortunately, it seems he has a sore leg."

"Yoo-hoo. Oh, honored master, sir." The leg problem suddenly disappears. "But can you walk?" asks the master. When Taro Kaja proves that he can indeed walk with ease, the master bellows: "Then go get the fish!" Just as suddenly the cramp comes back. The master glowers, Taro Kaja cowers, and the play ends with them walking off the stage single file, Taro Kaja following humbly.

Why the down denouement? Kyōgen was born in an era when the slightest disobedience to a lord was as likely to attract a slashing sword as a sharp word. Even onstage, it was not wise to poke too much fun at the ruling class.

"But what if Taro Kaja just runs off the stage," I suggested. It would have a sharper impact. Sensei would not consider any changes after none had been allowed for seven centuries. Not even the tiniest expressions were to be allowed. Remember, the eyes were to remain straight ahead at all times.

"You shouldn't even blink."

"That is impossible," I objected.

"Perfection is difficult. It is not meant to be achieved, but rather attempted."

"Don't you ever want to just let go? I mean, if we timed it right we could have them chuckling in their *obento* boxes."

"It is easy to make audience laugh. We want them to laugh and then go home and think."

I had a dream. I was on the Noh stage, but the stage reflected another stage, as two mirrors on opposite walls reflect each other into infinity. I was about to enter into the other stage when sensei said to me, "Don't act."

I told Juro about the dream. He made no comment.

The day of the performance finally arrived. By what I thought was chance but now believe was arranged by sensei, the other *deshi* who was scheduled to act beside me became mysteriously ill. Sensei took his place. It is unheard of for a professional actor to perform onstage with a mere student. I must have been, therefore, officially an *uchi deshi*.

For the first time, I was allowed backstage into the sacred room where Noh actors don their masks in front of a large mirror and take on the spirit of the god whose part they perform. There was no mask for my part.

I was presented with my costume, and sensei helped me dress. He tied the belt deliberately, precisely, as he did everything. He helped me slip into a vest with starched winglike projections for shoulders. Because of the difference in our heights, when I turned to say something I poked him in the eye with one of those shoulders.

And then suddenly it was time. We waited at the side of the stage, facing the closed vertical-striped, five-colored, embroidered-silk side curtain, *sensei* standing in front of me in front of the center gold stripe. My heart was pounding. I was light-headed. At the very last moment, sensei turned to me: "Don't act."

The dream!

The curtain opened. I couldn't breathe. My fixed eyes were like a camera on a dolly as I glided across the bridge and onto the stage. I watched myself moving from outside myself.

I did what I had been taught to do; my position was exact, my breath at the right moment. Something, however, was not going according to the way I had been taught. Sensei was pausing longer for laughs than he should have. He was acting; he was stealing the show. Instinctively I, too, started acting, and yet it was not me. The audience was rolling.

Then the end. I see my feet taking me across the bridge once more. The curtain closes behind me. I have just violated everything I have been taught for years, and it has been fun. The audience loves it. They are still applauding when sensei turns toward me.

When in doubt in Japan, apologize. *"Gomen nasai. I'm sorry,"* I said, without meaning it in the least.

His smile was glowing. "Yes." The apology had been necessary and unfelt. Perfect. Form had been maintained.

I had crossed the bridge not merely onto the Kyō-gen stage but, more important, into the world of traditional Japan that had previously appeared inaccessible to an outsider. I had walked in the footsteps of emperors and shoguns. I had spoken the words of ancient poets and playwrights.

Zeami, the man who set the standards for excellence in Noh and wrote most of the plays, once decreed that a play should have a tinge of unreality in order to better reveal the truth. Makes sense. For me, everything was tinged with unreality.

Putting on the Zen

Wide Eyes

·······························

I LEFT JAPAN BECAUSE I COULDN'T SEE MYSELF DYING THERE.
Actually, I couldn't see myself living there, either. My
teaching was becoming a routine—a successful stand-
up comic routine, but all the same, routine. I was a re-
placement cog, a *gaijin*. No one was talking to me as a
person. The first two minutes of any telephone conversation were preprogrammed. Variations were frowned
upon. It was enough to give Sisyphus a fit.

I was becoming hungry to see the world while I
still had health to do so. I was approaching thirty-two
years old. I figured I had about eight more years, fifteen
on the outside, to live. I developed a desire for travel

and photography from my acquaintance with an Irish-American I'll call Dan because that was his name. I remember vividly the moment we met.

During the get-acquainted social for new teachers at FLUK, a young man with red hair and a face also red comes rushing up to me angrily and hollers in my face, *"You're married?"*

I learned that my assailant, Dan, and his friend Kathy had applied for a job at the school and were asked if they were married. Since they were living together anyway and really needed the job, they decided to lie. Then they were told that FLUK didn't hire married couples: women would soon leave to have children, so they weren't worth training. After they pleaded for the school to reconsider, they were finally both allowed to work there, but only if they were willing to accept lower wages.

After we got to know each other, Mars and I were forgiven for being married, and we all became friends. Dan loved to go through back issues of *National Geographic,* drooling over the pictures of exotic places and dreaming of traveling there to take such photos.

I bought an Olympus camera under his influence. Dan and his photographer friends would have photo viewing parties where they would also critique my slides honestly, and often painfully.

I was shooting with him at Meiji Park the day I first put on my thirty-five millimeter lens, a wide-angle lens that takes in everything around you but makes it less important to concentrate on one particular thing straight ahead. I kept the camera to my eye for so many hours that day, that when I took it away, my consciousness stayed in the wide-angle mode. The streets of Tokyo transformed into a new reality. My personal space was magnified.

One day I found myself in busy Shinjuku station, where three million people pass through daily. Multiple exits from many subway lines and many more train lines gush passengers upstairs and pour them downstairs from every side into a large open lobby, a churning black-haired ocean of busy people crossing in all directions. Shuffling due to the lack of room to walk, they would form rivulets of three or four shufflers. For some reason I decided to go wide-angle.

Keeping my eyes directly ahead and unfocused, as in Kyōgen, I moved my foot toward a space about to become vacant, always maintaining balance. I glided across the lobby with ease. When I got to the other side, I couldn't believe that what had just happened had really just happened. I went back into the crowd and across the lobby and back, dancing through a multitude as if they or I were a mirage.

......

Dan and all of us would sit on the tatami floor, legs underneath the warm *kotatsu* table, drink green tea, listen to ethnic music, look at slides, and dream of traveling all around the world. By the time he left Japan years later, he had a route all planned out based on a cheap airline ticket from Egypt Air with many possible stops en route. At the end of our third year in Japan, I followed him. He was my travel guru, for he often told me how much he knew about various cultures, especially compared to me. His curiosity was inspiring. His knowledge was intimidating.

Mars and I caught up with him in Bali, April 1979. He was doing everything he could to become part of the culture and ridiculed me for being so other, so insensitive. He was wearing a sarong rather than pants or shorts. He wore a flower in his ear, alternating the ear each day to indicate one day that he was married and the next that he was not. He couldn't remember which ear meant which, but since he had lied about being married, it didn't really make any difference anyway. He loved everything about Bali; it was heaven to him.

To me, too. One day I returned to the quiet of our beautiful bungalow next to his, a little brick palace with a polished-stone porch and ever-available flowers and tea.

Dan was red-faced and fuming.

"They're laughing at me! Just because I try to fit into their culture. Not just laugh. They were shouting down the street and pointing at me so others wouldn't miss the show.

"Today I found this magnificent hat at the market. Cool. Look at the artistry in this simple, practical object. So refined. I know I can't be one of them. I cannot walk as straight as these people. They are trained from birth. They practice all their life, and it is beautiful. I can only wish to be that graceful. But the sad truth is, no matter how hard I tried I am screwed; I was not born to this culture, so the hat would not stay on my head. So I hooked up a chin strap. I think I did a passable job.

"I'm wearing this walking down the street, and people are running inside to bring the family out on the front porch to cackle at me because I need a chin strap. Pointing and howling and rolling on the floor and pounding the planks. It isn't that big of a thing, a chin strap! Mocking me for trying to respect them. It's humiliating. I don't have to take this kind of bull. I'm leaving this hole tomorrow."

It was about a week later that someone told him his new hat was really a bamboo rice steamer.

......

We often don't understand that we are looking at illusion in our own life. It is easier to see other peoples' illusions.

At dusk pedicab drivers, their passengers, and people on foot enter the gates and gather on the grass in front of the cloth screen where shadows dance to the exotic music of the Indonesian *wayang kulit* (shadow-puppet play).

A flash of light blanks the screen. An American tourist out of her element explains that her camera is automatic. It adjusts to the conditions and activates the flash only when necessary. It was obviously necessary.

Weeks later when she opens up her developed photos, only one picture will be damaged. Perhaps it had been mistakenly exposed to light during the development process? Funny, all the other photos turned out OK. What was it a picture of?

It is a Zen photo pointing out illusion. The shadow-puppet play is illusion. The shadows themselves are illusion. Trust in technology without understanding: illusion. Result: white.

I meander toward the other side of the curtain. I am naturally drawn backstage. I want to catch a glimpse of the *dalang* in action. A *dalang* is simultaneously a master puppeteer, storyteller, singer, orchestra leader, and shaman. He sees me and motions for me to take my shoes off and come up onto the stage behind the screen. He hands me two small mallets and encourages me to strike two fist-sized gongs in time with the man who sits beside me playing a similar set of gongs with higher tones.

The tempo is slow at first, quickens subtly, then explodes, and then . . . silence. I feel the crescendo, at one with the gong musician beside me. Silence. My gong gongs too long. Wrong!

The *dalang* is honest with me afterward: "The music of a beginner is painful to my ears."

We moved from Bali to Yogyakarta slowly on our world tour. We had found several out-of-the-way places mentioned in the independent traveler's bible for Indonesia, Bill Dalton's *Indonesian Handbook*. It so happened that Dalton was staying at a *losman,* a kind of cheap hostel with private rooms, right next to the *losman* where we were staying. I had never done anything like this before, but I went up to the author and complimented him on his book. We talked about some of the places I had visited at his suggestion, and he took notes. Apparently I had an eye for detail of which I was not conscious. At the end of the conversation I told him he ought to do a book about Japan. He countered, "Why don't you? I'd publish it if it's any good."

"I'll think about it. Got me a ticket right now, and I want to take as long as I can to complete the journey. Right now, I don't want to ever go back. I'll look you up when and if I return to the U.S."

Months later Mars and I met up with Dan and Kathy again in Delhi, from where we all took a train and then bused north to Kashmir and Srinagar, the village beside beautiful Dal Lake. Dan and Kathy coaxed us onto a bus ride to exotic Ladakh, or Lower Tibet, over Zoji La, an eleven-thousand-foot mountain pass.

We started our two-day, twelve-hour-each-day bus ride to Leh, the capital of Ladakh, from Srinagar. We had waited a month for the tickets and took the first seats that became available. We hoped we would make it there before the first snowfall, although it already was late August. I sat in the back of the bus by the window behind the wheels. A rattling back door was to the side of my right thigh.

We were off on an adventure of a lifetime, excited about what was to come. Crossing the Himalaya range by road!

Five minutes out of town we came to a bump in the pavement that threw me up, banging my head on the roof. My elbow came down on the back of Kathy's hand, for she had prudently grabbed on to the armrest next to me. We were both groaning in pain. *Two days of this! What had we gotten ourselves into?*

We climb into the hills along rivers, into the Himalayas. The road is an ever-turning line etched on the side of these grand mountains. At one point I look down on eagles flying over barley fields the size of postage stamps. The bus turns around a hairpin and begins up a steeper slope; the driver shifts down. The gears grind, don't take. We start going backward. I am cantilevered over the expanse of nothingness. Fear is grinding. Gears, still grinding, finally catch, and we lurch forward. I breathe. Exhausted. A dizzy rush of adrenaline. I had given myself up for dead, yet I'm still alive. Very alive. *My senses take on a patina of rich color like water paints on dry stone.*

Stars When the Sun Shines

The path clung to the ever-twisting edge of the steep mountain cliff, with the bus taking up most of the narrow road. Then around the corner we see an army truck appear. We will have to squeeze by on the outside of the one-and-a-half-lane road, the cliff-edge side. Another truck appears, and another.

Dan turns around to me, panic distorting his face, his flaming hair standing on end. *"It's a convoy!"* he screams in terror. His face reflects my feelings. He looks hilarious. I laugh in the face of death. Freedom.

Dan, needing a bathroom badly, struggled heroically.

I couldn't blame him for taking the opportunity when the bus stopped briefly to let some sheep cross the road. He jumped out the back door next to me and headed for some privacy. It took a very long time. When he got back on the bus, some European travelers let him know of their dismay. "The ride is already going to be twelve hours long today, man." "Yeah, like, get your stuff together, man."

Dan could have been more gracious and apologetic. Instead, he managed to escalate everything into name-calling and national slurs. The bus nearly became an international incident.

We had a long ride ahead, and the feeling on the bus was thick with people into their sentiments. I was angry with Dan, although I understood his plight, and I was angry with those who were angry with him, though

I could see that their patience was in tatters. Whose side was I on?

Wait. It is not necessary for me to make a choice. I don't need to take sides. I don't need to find a reason to justify anyone else's anger. I have enough of my own to take care of. I choose not to participate.

At the next rest stop, Dan was getting off through my door when a traveler up front took another verbal swipe at him. As was his nature, he turned up his anger and shot back in rebuttal. Meanwhile, he backed out of the door, off the bus, and into a pile of bovine waste. It was hilarious to everyone except Dan. His reaction was predictable.

There is precious little water in those mountain villages, so Dan couldn't clean up very well. He was even less popular for the rest of that day on the open-windowed ride through the cool high mountains. That bus stunk of karma.

......

Mars had been traveling with me until she became very sick in Kathmandu. I remember the pedicab ride we took to the travel agent to get her ticket home.

"Why not go someplace else? How about the Alps? 'From Annapurna to the Alps.' It's got a kind of ring to it. I am not ready to go home."

"I want to go home." This was not negotiable.

"Mars, remember how we made a promise to each other that we would not get in the way of the other

Stars When the Sun Shines

88

one's trip. Would you be well enough to get home by yourself?" She was brave.

And so I was alone on my journey. I had been doing toe-touching stretches because it is a great deal easier to travel when you are in shape. In Japan I had become fat and unphysical. I could only reach halfway down my shins when I left. So every morning for a few minutes I would bend at the hip and hang my hands down to my comfort level until it slowly started to stretch out. The day after Mars left, my hands touched my toes and stayed there for as long as I wished.

When I stood up, I became aware of this thin man staring at me through a window where a mirror had once been. I had taken a dislike of thin men because they seemed like a judgment about my being fat. So I took an immediate and automatic dislike of this A-hole peeking in on me.

"Wait a minute. That *is* a mirror. That's me. I have lost this much weight? Looks like I'm going to need to adjust my attitude." I went up and forced myself to look in the mirror until we made friends. That guy in the mirror wasn't perfect, but then neither was I.

I have developed the habit over the years that when I am feeling depressed and having existential questions about my self-worth, I force myself to go to a mirror and stare at myself in disgust. I mean, I really try to hate me. Depending on how down I am on me, in a short while I find myself laughing at that ridiculous face.

Wide Eyes

Someone told me that I am lucky because I was given a sense of humor.

"What? You don't have a mirror in your house?"

There is something to be said for three months with the runs—not a recommended, but a very effective, weight remover. This made it easy for me to make a decision when I came across a freshly butchered goat hanging covered with a gray cloak of flies. OK! No more meat! With that decision my anger lightened and also my weight. My stride increased. My energy. I felt I could do anything I put my mind to.

One day I rented a bicycle to ride to the outskirts of Kathmandu to do the tourist thing at Boudhanath Stupa. On the way, a woman in a vibrant sari, magenta on saffron, stood in front of a red-brown brick wall. Stunning. I stopped and grabbed my camera just as another traveler closer to her popped up with his camera almost in her face. She turned away.

Leave her alone, I thought, irritated at him for being so insensitive.

"But Wayne. You were about to take that same picture." It was the judge who had caught me judging.

"Yes. I was going to take that picture," I admitted. "But I have a telephoto lens."

"But the truth is, she doesn't want her picture taken. She probably is afraid of someone stealing her soul."

"I'm not taking her soul when I take her picture. I am not taking anything. I am honoring her beauty. If she doesn't know it is being taken, what is the big deal?"

"But the truth is, she didn't want her picture taken. You are just as bad as that traveler with the camera in her face."

"Get off my case, judge. I'm doing the best I can." And the judge was silenced; the sky became wider, bluer. I changed to the extra-wide-angle lens on my camera and in my mind.

......

My plane ticket brought me to Egypt, and a whim took me to Abu Simbel, an ancient temple located on the southern border. We flew from Cairo to the runway five miles from the famous Temple of the Dawn. For the first time on the whole trip, I was traveling with a tour group because it was the only affordable way to reach this remote temple. Predictably, I was annoyed about being tended like sheep in a flock by the bored tour guide.

"On your left you will notice the cartouche of Queen Necrophilia . . ." I blanked her out.

I couldn't sense the magic of the place despite its grandeur and antiquity. Though dwarfed by the awesome proportions of the hewn-stone statues, I was left numb, disappointed. So when the group was herded back onto the bus, I told the guide to go on without me.

"Don't be ridiculous, young man. You come along now. It is five miles across burning desert to the airport," she warned me. I was stubborn; I would find my own way back to the airport, I assured her. Thank you. The guide threw up her hands in disgust and left with the bus.

Finally, I am alone to absorb the magic, the majesty of the temple—alone except for three gawking unwelcoming Arabs in flowing *galabia* gowns who squat beneath the only shade tree in sight. The doors leading to the temple interior have been closed and locked, so I roam outside among the ancient carved stone. Four colossal figures of the mighty pharaoh Ramses II sit in a row flanking the entrance to the sacred chamber. One of the huge heads lies on the ground at the feet.

I begin to absorb the history of the temple. What an amazing feat of astronomical engineering! I can picture the pomp and pageantry of the ceremony, with bald priests and royalty in towering wigs. It is now dawn on the longest day of the year many millennia ago, a moment when the first ray of the rising solstice sun stabs into the center of a sanctified rock deep in the cavern. It is extremely Freudian.

I begin to feel the heat of the midday sun hammering down on the back of my neck—time to take refuge in the relative comfort of some shade. I find a niche for myself, literally: a tiny cleft with enough shade to crawl into. I decide to pass through this zone of white hotness by writing a letter to Mars: "I am sitting here in the shade . . ."

I stop, look around. Something is missing. I unfold myself from that niche and walk a short distance to another shade, sit down, and continue my letter: " . . . in the shade of the fallen head of Ramses II. A few moments ago I was sitting in a different shade, the first niche that I happened to come across; but by moving only a few steps, my words and my reality have suddenly taken on a larger significance.

"Here in the shelter of Ramses' shadow I have become one with the long history of this temple. I connect with these symbols of the Great Pharaoh's pride, symbols of his divinity and his absolute power. I also see it all now crumbling into ruin, humbled, the mighty power worn down to sand by the battering storms of time as in Shelley's poem 'Ozymandias.'

"How easily life passes and, therefore, what a great and precious treasure is this moment. It dawns on me here at the Temple of the Dawn that my recent journey of a few steps was a profound one from the ordinary acceptance of whatever happens to a moment infused with poignancy, this moment charged with metaphors of universal principles. I have consciously walked toward the poetic; I am romancing my life. Could I do this more often? Could I fill every moment of my life with such poetry?

"Yes! I could at least give it a shot. What's to lose?"

Shade of Poetry

A casual traveler in an antique land,
I chanced upon the Temple of the Dawn,
Carved out of stone by Pharaoh King's command
To mark the rising of the solstice sun.

Four colossal Pharaohs sit enthroned,
His majesty forever to proclaim.
The mountain shook; a giant head was thrown
And lying at his feet it now remains.

The sun was at its peak; I went for shade,
But chose to walk a few more steps instead.
Although the sunlight stabbed me like a blade,
I made it to the shadow of his head.

For though it was but just another shade,
I fathomed all the poetry we made.

Eating the Wind

I FINALLY CONTACTED THE PUBLISHER BILL DALTON about a year after our talk in Java, only to discover that he had suggested the idea of a book on Japan to another writer, a friend of his who had taken it on. I blew the chance for a book. Now what was I going to do?

"Why don't you do a guidebook on China? It's just starting to open up."

So Mars and I went to San Francisco, holed up in a cheap share-the-bath hotel near Union Square, and went to the library to start learning about China. We were poring over piles of books in our room when I came upon one about Thailand.

I scolded Mars for her lack of focus. We had enough to read already with China. I mean, China, Mars? Think how huge this is. But I read the book on Thai history out of curiosity and then called Mr. Dalton.

"How about a book on Thailand instead?" I suggested.

"How about a book on all of Southeast Asia?" he countered. What would that entail? Thailand, Burma, Malaysia including Borneo, Singapore, Brunei, and the Philippines—not all 7,107 of the islands, I was assured. Since they were right on my way I could throw in Hong Kong and Macau if I liked. And Bill would loan me his notes on Indonesia—not all 17,508 islands, of course— so we could get the book out sooner. He offered me a cash advance.

For a first book, this project was way too big. We took a deep breath, and in June 1980, about seven months after I had returned to the States from the spin round the world, we flew off to Southeast Asia once more in what was to be the first of many trips I took as a writer. We had no idea how we were going to do whatever it was we were going to do.

Mars came along with me on that first research trip but returned to the U.S.A. to find a home for us somewhere while I hitched across the section of Borneo that had roads. It was during that part of the trip that I realized that the truth about travel for me couldn't be found in a guidebook format. Guidebooks, in fact, were a barrier between the traveler and his or her own unique experience.

I loved to travel as much as possible without a plan, without a schedule, with only a map to dream on and with chance as my guide. I lived on the edge, tightrope walking without a net, no support group, gambling my limited money reservoir on a few more months on the road, at times without a home, no shared culture or language, on my own. Total attention at all times was essential for survival. Life was alive and exciting inside the moment, and I found myself helping those around be in this moment with me. I was the movie. Life became a traveling celebration.

My publisher, Bill Dalton, picked me up from the San Francisco airport on my return. I was excited to share these ideas with him about where my book was heading and did so during the trip home. He drove off the road, barely avoiding an accident. Should have waited till we were back to Chico.

The first draft of my first book was a fiasco. To save the little money we had, I wrote it on the back of tax-return forms I found at the post office. The writing didn't deserve any better paper. I had been looking for the wrong information. I was telling people about the cost and quality of cheap hotels, to turn left at the Coca-Cola sign, rather than describing the excitement of the night market in Chiang Mai or the awesomeness of arriving by outrigger with the full moon gleaming phosphorescence on the white sands of Boracay. It was no longer possible to use Bill's notes on Indonesia. I was looking for something different—wanting to find, insisting on uncovering, the essence.

I had heard about an ancient meditation cave located near Parangtritis, on the southern coast of Java, from a Buddhist man named Ecco Legowo, who was studying agriculture in Chico. The cave has been a sacred place of pilgrimage and meditation for fifteen hundred years, since the time of the ancient Hindu-Buddhist kingdom of Mataram. The spirits of the cave are even older. Going there is a chance to touch the core of the Javanese soul.

Ecco told us that the path to the cave was quite difficult, but that his father, the venerable Bapak, would be glad to guide us if we wished to go. Ecco had been there many times in his youth, even slept there on a terrace beside cobras. "No problem if you do not show fear."

From Yogyakarta in central Java we went south to the coast—Bapak, Mars, and I. We waded across a shallow river to the other bank for the final mile, entering the village of Parangtritis at twilight. The next morning I looked at the stormy, sunny beach where swimming is not advised. Waves come pounding unobstructed all the way north from Antarctica. The sea is a roiling green seething of waves that reach far inland on that shallow shoal. Wind picks up sand and blasts any plant or being that dares get in its way.

Stars When the Sun Shines

A local tradition has this sea inhabited by Loro Kidul, a sorceress who was once spurned by the sultan and as a consequence must be appeased annually with offerings of the current sultan's yearly hair and nail clippings, considered extremely magical in these parts.

Job description: you must collect and keep safe His Majesty's nail removals as well as any and all hair removals. Apply with references.

People drown diving after the clippings for good fortune. Loro Kidul lures lovers to her palace beneath the waves and seduces males, especially those who wear her favorite color, green. The place feels as if it is seething with spirits.

I was soaking in a large pool fed by the soothing waters of a natural hot spring on the inland side of the village. Late in the morning, Bapak came to ask if I wished to go to the cave. If we started soon, it should take only five hours.

Five hours. Good news. We will be back in time for sunset.

No, he corrected me; it would take us five hours just to get there. It would take him, a man of sixty, only a few hours if he were alone, he admitted humbly. *Lead on, old man,* I challenged him in my mind. I was fit and could handle the hike. Mars was just as fit. We would hardly be a drag on him.

He walked as if his feet weren't quite touching the land, without effort, as if he were merely willing himself forward, uphill—floating, even though his feet really did touch the ground. I checked.

I earned each one of my steps and paid twice as much in energy on every slope. My knee was screaming. After about four hours in the sun, we came to an open-sided but roofed platform with a woven-bamboo floor, a cooling place for rice harvesters, where Bapak suggested we take a rest.

"I'm fine," I said competitively. "How much farther to the cave?"

About half an hour.

"So let's go on and rest in the cave, unless you're tired."

"I am fine. You need to rest here," he insisted.

Maybe Mars does, I thought. He was our host, and he was telling us to take a nap. I never liked nap time. We compliantly stretched out on the pliant bamboo floor of the platform. I defiantly kept my eyes open.

A local man who had recently been blown out of his fragile hut came by. He and his family had moved into the cave, our destination, until they could build another hut. They had no money at the moment for such a dream.

"That is excellent," says Bapak. "They will cook our meal tonight. Leaf curry. Otherwise we would have fasted."

"I didn't know that!"

"Give him your camera bag. He will carry it for you."

Stars When the Sun Shines

Besides my camera, the bag contained my plane ticket, passport, travelers checks, and, most precious of all, my writing notes. Was this some kind of scam? Or perhaps it was a test to see if I really trusted him and was, therefore, trustworthy? In any event, I had learned not to argue with Bapak. I gave up my bag, and the man disappeared with it.

A few minutes later we followed Bapak through a narrow cleft in the rock. We came into a small open area walled in by steep boulders on all sides, with a triangular rock in the center like a miniature pyramid. Bapak knelt down and prayed out loud, bowing in the Muslim fashion.

I thought that if this rock had any spirits they would be able to hear the skepticism in my voice, so I decided to talk to it telepathically instead. It wasn't that I really believed. The rock just seemed to be the gatekeeper.

"Let's pretend like you really have some say in this whole thing, Mr. Rock. On that condition I would certainly appreciate that you bless the rest of our journey." I said amen out of an old habit.

I have a feeling the church doesn't approve of rock worship. I asked Bapak later how it was that he, a Muslim, felt it was OK to pray to a rock. He responded, "Allah made the rock."

We squeezed through another cleft beyond that big little pyramid, and the world dropped away. From a dizzying height I could see the green water far below with waves crashing against the rocky coast, waves

hungrily climbing over the rocks, reaching up like grab-
bing hands.

There was a bamboo ladder, thank God! I could handle that. Bapak went first, Mars followed, and I brought
up, or rather down, the end. At the bottom of the long
springy ladder was a ledge on which we edged our way
to another ladder, thank God! I kept both hands firmly
on the rungs tied with homemade twine. I looked down.
The waves rose high to get me, but I was still far above.
If only I can maintain this distance.

Another ledge. I expected another ladder but was
disappointed. O God! Instead the land had been notched
for finger and toeholds. The local people are quite a bit
shorter than I am, so when I went to find the first step, it
was a foot higher than I would have preferred. I bent my
waist, thrusting my butt awkwardly far from the cliff edge
and pulling me with it. My fingers tore into the land. No
way would I have survived with my camera bag on.

I changed plans. Instead, I stretched to feel for the
next niche farther down, skipping the immediate one,
extending fully from the tips of my fingers to the tip of
my toe.

I looked down. The waves were saying, *"Come to me,
come to me."* It was Loro Kidul. These pants are olive, not
really green. I quibbled. *"Come to me, Wayne. Come. You
can fly. You can fly."*

"No I can't! No I can't!" I countered and clung on
for dear life. I didn't look down again but rather kept

my face fiercely concentrating on the earth in front of my nose. I kept my nose so close to that earth that I was cross-eyed in concentration and didn't realize that the slope had changed. Peripherally I glimpsed four strange-looking trees standing next to the path as I backed past them on level ground. Two of the trees were wearing pants. Bapak.

My fear had been exposed; I felt humiliated by my cowardliness in front of my wife and a respected old man. To make matters more disturbing, we were heading to a cave with cobras where it would be no problem as long as I didn't show my fear. What were the chances of that? I did not feel at the top of my game.

Bapak made no comment, showed no reaction. Perhaps he was merely being Asian, not showing his thoughts on his face. We continued to the cave.

There were no cobras because the family had moved in.

The father proudly hands me my tote bag with a smile. Everything intact, I'm sure. I don't dare check my bag in front of him. His family will survive because of the small tips we will give him. He is grateful for whatever he receives.

We each took a shower one at a time in spring water channeled through bamboo on the inside wall of the cave lobby. The others waited at the mouth of the cave and watched the hungry waves crash upon the rock in the light of the waning sun.

Eating the Wind

Then Bapak led us into the cave. A stalagmite formed a rounded stairway, allowing us to crawl up the three steps as an infant just learning to climb stairs. At the top we waded across a small room with milky water on the floor, ankle deep. My feet were invisible. We came to a narrow passageway about four feet wide with an archway of stalactites that we needed to duck under to pass through. You were either humble or you had a headache. Bapak warned us that there was no floor here and to be careful to locate the log that had been wedged invisibly about a foot beneath the surface of the milky water. We balanced, bowing, through the arched channel on an invisible bridge.

Finally we reach the inner chamber, a room with a very low ceiling and a floor that slants at an extreme angle. At the lower end is a spring from which water gurgles, sounding eerily like a human voice. In addition, almost rhythmically I can feel the pressure rather than hear the sound of those crashing waves detonating upon the Java coast outside the cave.

Bapak had lit our way with a flashlight. Now he turns it off. It is dark. I imagine I see light to my side. I look. It disappears. To my other side?

"OOOoooooom!" Bapak's quiet voice has taken on surprising strength, a fullness of tone that fills the cave and then . . . silence. Except for the babbling spring and the non-noise compression of the crashing waves. Silence.

The voice of the spring. What is it saying? Imagine what it is saying. *"Ask any questions you want."*

Ask any question you want? What question would you ask? Is there a question that should be asked?

Eventually it became clear to me that the only question that is worth asking on a cosmic level is the one where I feared the answer. I was too afraid of my cancer and death to ask about that. But I was wondering if climbing down cliffs and traveling around Asia on the rough and writing books about places I knew little about was such a good idea even if it gave me a chance to be a writer. So I asked, "Am I supposed to, to be a writer?"

"Yes."

Thank God!

"But you're writing the wrong book. Go ahead. You must finish the book you are now planning to write. But it is not the book you are supposed to write."

We returned to the village the next afternoon. Bapak introduced us to his great-aunt, a blind faith healer who was rumored to be 136 years old. She hugged both Mars and me with amazing strength. When she heard that we had been to the meditation cave, she hugged us again; she was so happy for us to have had that experience. Come to think of it, that second hug may have been more of a blessing.

"I haven't been to cave for, oh, it must be fifty years now," said the frail old woman. "Not since they put in the path."

......

Eating the Wind

I returned the advance money to Bill and gave up the rights to write *Southeast Asia Handbook*. I couldn't write to the assignment. It wasn't in me. But it was impossible for me to give up the dream of writing a book once I'd committed myself to doing so. Mars joined me for the ride. She would be the publisher.

Somehow, with a perseverance my brother Paul labeled obsessive and others have called stubbornness and manic delusion, we managed to manifest the first book: *Wide Eyes in Burma and Thailand: Finding Your Way*. The hint of a spiritual journey was intentional, but the ideas were not yet developed. The final graphic in the book, a cartoon, shows a traveler on a *wagon* looking at the *stars*. (That was in 1982, long before I learned what my name means in 2006.)

In the story that goes with the cartoon, the traveler, me, has lost all his belongings. Metaphorically speaking, I certainly had. But the real story wasn't mine. It was actually that of a friend who had all his gear stolen, including his prized Hasselblad camera. The rest of the story was what I imagined it would be like to be stripped of almost everything. Instead of this being a problem, I am excited about the upcoming adventure: "Who knows what is going to come my way? I'm ready for the ride."

......

Our time for research was often extremely limited, but especially in Burma. It was Burma then. It is Burma now. We were allotted only seven days per visit, and I wished to write about this country? How? Do what you can. Don't do what you can't.

On our second trip to Burma, Mars and I split up to cover as much ground as we possibly could in the short span of time we had. She continued on the train from Rangoon north with our friend Teresa to Mandalay, and I jumped off at Thazi Station in order to go to Inle Lake, located in the Shan hill country five hours due east.

The jeep overloaded with nine passengers. The driver stopped to add a couple more to our crowd. I made a joke of my discomfort and suggested that he stop for some more people, for many stood by the road waiting for rides. Waving my sarcasm away, smiling, and pointing up ahead, he laughed and said something I didn't understand.

We have been bouncing along the dusty road for forty-five minutes when I become aware of the sun on my back. The sun rises in the east. The sun is behind me. *We are going west!*

It seems he had arranged to pick someone up in that direction first, and then we would continue back to Inle. We had just added two hours to an uncomfortable five-hour journey.

An hour in the wrong direction! A wankin' waste of time. Two hours more of bouncing and cramping in a crowded, bumpy jeep. I am furious.

We come to a rest stop. I walk across the road kicking rocks up over a rise in my frustration—my anger about to break out of its fragile control—when I come to the crest and look down upon a cobalt lake mirroring the clear blue sky. In the middle of the lake is a barely visible peninsula leading to a golden temple built upon the water. Reflecting up, reflecting down. Stunning!

It is not a place you can get to if you are going there. You arrive as a gift. Thank you. My anger suddenly looks foolish, a bigger waste of time and energy than many hours of jeep travel. Just because I have a reason to be angry doesn't mean I have to be. Unless, of course, I want to enjoy being angry.

I felt as if I had been brought to this place in spite of myself. Reflecting down, reflecting up. That's what a portal looks like, the golden door to new dimensions. Thank you.

Slow down. Set your watch back thirty minutes from Bangkok time and your mind back a century. The Buddhists of Burma believe that to hurry is to show a lack of trust in fate—a sure sign of insufficient merit for the good life. Here in this human sanctuary, speed has been filtered out of time. It is always now, and it feels like forever.

Don't take your time. Leave it on the plane seat when you get off at Rangoon.

......

I enter a Thai *wat,* a temple dedicated to Buddha. Gautama Buddha asked that no images be made in his memory. The request has been ignored dramatically, for I now pass a long row of Buddhas, each one varying slightly from the one before. I walk along the statues until I come to one that attracts my eye. I don't know why. I sit down on the floor in front of this statue, my legs folded behind me. I imitate the expression on this Buddha's face. *Have I ever felt like this?*

I was four years old, playing on the steps that lead up to the bath and the boys' and girls' bedrooms on the second floor of our home. The stairs were a zig with a window on the landing where mom had some small potted plants on glass shelves. That is where my farmer-and-corn-cob pot sat with a cactus growing from it, I believe. I never really paid attention to anything in the pot except the very important fact that I had my very own farmer-and-corn-cob planter.

I was having a great giddy time chasing a Slinky down the stairs and running into the next room squealing. Only that day I couldn't go into the living room. The door was closed because Miss Wiggins, who came from the "cities," was giving piano lessons. She was offered a place to stay overnight in the living room on the pullout sofa and the use of the piano to bring in other paying students in return for teaching, or rather trying to teach, us five children piano. I was pre-Wiggins age, but I was intrigued at what was going on through that strangely closed door.

Reverend P. J. came over for a unplanned visit. He was an honored guest at our house, for he had baptized Dad, confirmed both Mom and Dad, and performed their marriage ceremony. He had been minister at Belle

Plaine St. Johannes Kirche for forty-seven years. He was now widowed, and, of course, he was always welcome to come over for a chat and stay for lunch, "if you insist."

He loved my brother Paul, who was well behaved in church. Also, they had the same initials in their name. *So what?* thought I, dismissing the coincidence until I found out that I shared mine with William Shakespeare.

I am avoiding the horrible thing that happened to me. My Slinky did it again. *How can it do that?* I wondered. I run down the stairs and into the kitchen squealing and meet God scowling. Holy *sh!* Don't say it.

"Children should be seen, and not heard."

Mom whisks the offending urchin from the sight of God's wrath, puts me on the steps, and commands with a frown that I play here, quietly. Then, horror of horrors, the door to the kitchen is closed. I'm trapped on both sides. I am all alone. I am in prison. Solitary confinement.

I tried not to. I tried to play with the Slinky, but it had lost its bounce. I tried not to cry. The Slinky failed again.

My whimpers are halted when the light changes in my staircase corridor. A golden light pours down over me from the window in the landing, the window facing north in Minnesota, a window that never before or since has received sunlight. A voice says, *"Wait, Wayne. Wait. This will all make sense, someday. You are blessed."*

I find myself getting cramped legs on the cool floor of a Thai temple and looking at a row of Buddhas. Did I fall asleep?

Stars When the Sun Shines

......

I was hitchhiking, waiting for a ride alongside the two-lane highway that meanders down the east coast of the Malayan Peninsula. I stood in the hot afternoon sun for a moment without moving a step, standing right where I waved good-bye to the previous ride.

I have two rules for hitching. The first: *you never get a ride until you are happy where you are.* I decided to hike a half mile from the sun to some shade. I wouldn't be happy getting badly sunburned again.

"If you do feel dizzy from the sun, put your head between your knees and eat some juicy fruit. Not necessarily at the same time." I wrote this advice in the *Wide Eyes* book, and I remembered it, laughing, as I made my way to the shade.

Across the road a young woman in a sarong leans over on a ladder and energetically scrapes paint from the side of her house. To balance each stroke, her rounded behind undulates under the tightness of the sarong.

A white car with air conditioning.

What? Oh! Not now!

Your ride, Wayne. A white car with air conditioning.

I look up the road and see a white car with windows closed coming around the corner where I had been a while ago. My second rule of hitching: *if you are asking chance for a ride, you have to take whatever ride chance brings.* I glance back at the shapely young woman.

Eating the Wind

My eyes are drawn again to the white car. I do not raise a hand; I don't move. I just stand there looking. The car slows, pulls over, stops, the door opens, a whiff of sandalwood. A dark Indian man looking disturbed, without a smile: "Get in. I want you to know, I never stop for hitchhikers but something told me to stop for you."

"I don't know what is happening, but I knew you were coming."

We talked about what we both had just experienced, reaching no conclusion but having a strengthened feeling of fate or perhaps, less fearfully, of destiny. He read my palm. I have an unusually strong and straight destiny line, he told me as I nervously watched the road he wasn't looking at. I didn't really believe in palm reading, but I indulged him. He went an extra hundred kilometers—thank you!—to take me to the door of a friend I had met on a previous trip, where I planned to stay the night.

The next day a young neighbor woman happened by in her car while my host of the night before and I were waiting for a bus. She offered us a ride into town. I sat beside her in front.

I knew this woman. I had met her three years earlier at a village festival in a small town a long ways north of here on a previous trip hitching the east coast. At that time she was a teenage princess who was being forced to marry her sultan uncle rather than the rock star she loved. I was fascinated and curious as to how things would turn out. I asked her at that time to write me a letter and let me know what happened. She promised me she would, but never did.

"You owe me a letter." She recognized me immediately. Turns out she married the uncle and got a divorce. No mention of the rock star.

Eating the wind. That is what the Indonesians call travel. I love it. I love to feel the wind against my face, to stand up in the back of a pickup and let the breeze massage me, to travel always hungry for more. And more.

......

On the other side of the peninsula, a police paddy wagon stops while I am hitching. I wasn't sure if hitching was legal or not. I suspected not. I walk slowly toward them. Two turbaned policemen look through their rolled-down window at me.

"Are you hitching or are you not? Where are you going? Penang? That is on our way, lah. Get in."

Take the ride that is offered. I get in the back, where the windows are screened with heavy metal. I am locked in and uncomfortably practicing trust. A few hours later we come to a Y in the road where my destination, Penang, veers from theirs, Alor Setar. It is raining. The Sikh policemen invite me to come along with them and spend part of the night at a card party.

"We gamble only for pennies, isn't it?"

The next morning I discover that I have overstayed my visa by way too many days to be comfortable. I need to get to the immigration office immediately and will almost certainly have to pay a bribe I can ill afford. My new friend the policeman escorts me through the swinging wooden gate leading directly to the office of the head customs official and makes sure I receive special treatment, no charge. I was his guest, after all. This in Malaysia, where they used to stamp the visa of independent travelers with "S.H.I.T." in large letters: Suspected Hippy In Transit.

A lawyer friend of mine, an Englishman named Humphrey Ball, who became a Malaysian citizen when the nation was founded in the fifties, told me he didn't mind having to pay bribes at all: "At least you know what you are getting for your money. Don't think of it as a bribe. Think of it as a way to relate to the government on a personal level."

As a lawyer Humphrey could find no validity in the concept of intellectual property. Ideas, he thought, belong to everybody. I couldn't argue with him. I wasn't quite sure I owned any of mine exclusively. It was as if there were a dimension where ideas exist outside of material stuff you can knock a fist upon.

Plato's heaven would be in such a dimension. Plato described mankind as like unto cavemen chained to a position facing a wall. The only thing they can see is the dancing shadows on the wall. They have elaborate theories and debates about the nature of reality based on these shadows. After much haggling they have begrudgingly come to a consensus with limited variations, which they have agreed not to mention in each other's presence.

Then Plato's hero, a philosopher of course, breaks free from the chains of convention. He sees the fire and realizes how laughably shallow is shadow pedantry. The colorless shadows are not the thing at all. They are merely poor representations of the flickering fire.

Super philosopher person notices a bright light in the distance at the mouth of the cave. He sees immediately how dim is this artificial firelight and is drawn toward the brightness. At the mouth of the cave the world unfolds in glorious colors: greens, reds, blues, magenta, cinnabar, fuchsia, tangerine.

I understand reality as it really is. Not as I imagine it to be. I understand as I walk out into this magnificent new world being born for me in that moment. I am out of the shade, stepping into this wondrous golden light. What light is it?

I turn my eyes upward toward the source of all, and *I'm blind.*

This is the problem with enlightenment. All distinctions disappear. You can't see them because the light is too bright. Wayne's ego finds this very uncomfortable.

......

The first book, *Wide Eyes in Burma and Thailand,* exploded into more pages than I had imagined. We had already done much of the research on Malaysia, so I immediately began writing *Time Travel in the Malay Crescent*. I wanted it to be impressionistic travel where events get arranged inside of the reader's mind rather than being reported by me, a book that also shows how time disappears inside of the moment when one is really on the road at the edge.

I wrote while Mars published and meanwhile gathered graphics, maps for me to copy, and background information on future chapters. Mars did her research at California State University at Chico. They have an excellent map department.

She had searched the whole day for a map of the city of Alor Setar, a map I felt I desperately needed for the book, yet she returned empty-handed. She had not been able to find it.

"Now what am I going to do?" I asked rhetorically. I had just run across a great excuse for writer's block.

"You're going to come with me to do the laundry. We've got clothes that need washing."

Her argument was irrefutable, so I joined her. I was busy separating the whites from the colors when I noticed a strange pink piece of paper on the floor, like a page torn out of a cheap comic book. I bent over to pick it up in order to throw it away so nobody would slip on it.

A map of Alor Setar! Impossible. What is a map of a tiny town in northwestern Malaysia doing on the floor of a laundromat in northern California?

"All you have to do is ask."

Stars When the Sun Shines

Something or someone is helping me. How could I doubt any longer? Yet the truth is, I managed to find reasons to doubt and needed several reminders. Every time I grasped the concept, it would immediately start seeping through my fingers like water.

I found my writer's voice with my second book and lost it before the book was finished. I had a severe case of writer's block. Humbling as it is to admit, it is merely one huge ego trip. I didn't have confidence in my research, having missed the most important place historically in Malaysia, the old town of Malacca. We had a limited amount of money remaining from Japan, yet I was able to convince Mars and myself that yet another trip to Asia, less than a year after our previous one, was essential. We would go to work somewhere when the money ran out.

For some reason, I imagined an old man telling the story for the Malacca part of my book. The Old Man of Malacca. I couldn't get the image out of my mind.

After our flight landed in Hong Kong, we waited on the plane while the person seated next to us left and a new passenger arrived. The man was elderly, large, tall, tawny. He put his arm around and caressed the stewardess in a not entirely avuncular manner. In a booming voice, "Honey. Bring me a whiskey and water. Easy on the water."

He sat down. I made room by necessity. He turned to me. "You drink whiskey? Sure you do. Make that two, OK, honey."

Oh great! My thoughts sarcastic. *Asking a flight atten-dant for a drink before the flight begins, and in economy class. Who does this guy think he is? This is going to be a long flight. I'm sure the lovely Asian stewardess is going to stay as far away from us as possible.*

The stewardess returns with two drinks and bows when she serves them. It's as if she knows this man.

"Bless you, child," he says to her. To me: "And what is your name, sir?" I tell him and he sings my name: "Wayne Stier. John Wayne. I am pleased to meet you.

"My name is Lancelot. No, wait. I am told I must say it all. My name is Father Sir Lancelot Rodriguez. The 'Father' is supposed to come before the 'Sir,' did you know? I didn't know that. Where are you bound?"

I told him of the book I was writing and sheepishly admitted I was looking for a voice grounded in an imagi-nary old man of Malacca. Malacca? Sir Lancelot was from the Portuguese Settlement of Malacca. That was his desti-nation. He was attending the one-year anniversary of his mother's passing. I was invited to the get-together. "I'll introduce you to several old men. But I warn you: a lot of them, like me, haven't quite grown up yet."

During the five-hour flight I picked up the airline magazine and paged through it, looking at and critiqu-ing the pictures, trying to read some of the stories. They needed a writer.

Father Sir Lancelot was surprised when I showed up at his party unexpected, for invitations to strangers aren't commitments, but he graciously ushered me into the living room of his childhood home and introduced me to some old men. They do indeed like a good party.

That night a thunderstorm came over after sunset, and Lancelot insisted on going down to the seawall and far out on the pier to watch. "I miss these storms. Thunder and lightning. We don't have these kind of storms in Macau." Father Sir Lancelot was in charge of Catholic charities for Chinese based in Macau. He was talented at getting millionaires to donate to his cause, but he missed his boyhood home of Malacca.

Lightning flashed again. Sahb, another Portuguese from the Settlement who wouldn't leave us, shook his head: "Why? Why always that island? Why don't the lightning hit the other islands? They are taller. Only that one."

"Are you sure?" I asked.

"Course I sure. You call me a liar. I fish these waters."

That's odd, I thought. *The land here is red. It must have a great deal of iron in the rock. Iron resists energy flow. Lightning always takes the easiest path. Lightning has no reason to strike that island unless . . .*

......

In K.L.— Kuala Lumpur—I stopped at the head office for Malaysian Airlines to visit the editor of their magazine, *Wings of Gold.* What did I have to lose? I suggested a story about the Portuguese community in Malacca, and the idea was accepted. But I would have to supply slides along with my story.

I was on assignment. I could no longer afford the luxury of writer's block.

That was 1982, five years after I had decided to become a writer on that beach of Matabunkai Bay. I was selling my writing to someone who didn't know me. Someone actually chose to publish my writing, not just my wife, and also they wanted my photographs.

I even get paid! I am a writer.

In truth it had taken me five years before I had given myself a chance by even approaching an editor.

And thus began a period where I would go where chance and curiosity led me. I traveled to take photos and to write, and the money from that supported my continued budget travels. I dove off the cliff of chance hoping for safe water below, or perhaps to develop the ability to fly. Not every landing was an easy one, but they all worked out.

Fly into Thailand around midnight, too late to make it worth renting a room for a few hours. Instead find a ride to the southern bus station. Can't read the signs. Don't speak but a few words. Hop on the first bus that's leaving. Hand over a chunk of money. Conductor takes what he needs, hands the rest back. Lights of rural Thailand stream by, pointing out the darkness of the countryside. Golden temple spires lit against the black sky.

The bus stops. I mime sleep and poverty to the *trisha* peddler, and he takes me to a cheap hotel. I was using mime more often than words; in many cases it seems to have communicated better.

A few days later I discover I have chanced upon a village very near one of the last water markets flourishing in Thailand.

Sold photos and an article from this serendipitous discovery, which paid for some future travel.

My photographs were helping me to sell my writing, and the opposite was true as well. One of my photos made the cover of Singapore Airlines' *Silver Kris Magazine*. I also had the lead story, called "The Kyōgen Bridge."

Life is good.

......

I would return to the States, write up some articles, work on a book, and get ready to travel again within a year or at most two. The first time I returned from an around-the-world trip, I was sitting in the living room squirming from the lack of movement, lack of wind on my face, being back in the home where I had always been. My mother came into the room, recognized what I was going through, and went out of the room humming. I recognized the tune: *"How you gonna keep 'em down on the farm, after they've seen Paree?"* Mom, you are so right. I could no longer go home.

A recurring pattern developed as I roamed Southeast Asia. I would get the feeling that there might be a story for me to write in a village I knew nothing about. I would do what research I could, collect names to contact if possible, and go to the town with a loose plan. Inevitably, every lead I had dreamed up would prove fruitless, or the people I planned to meet were "out station." By late afternoon I'd begin to question the whole idea of squeezing an article out of this turnip of a town. I would bitterly give up and decide to enjoy a cool beer and some noodles instead.

You never get a ride until you are happy where you are. Immediately, my luck changed.

I began going into a town with a simpler plan: to sit at a stall, have myself a tea and snack, and watch the story unfold for me. Inevitably the man next to me would turn out to be a shadow-puppet master, a museum curator, a knowledgeable historian, a guide to a hidden temple.

......

In the matriarchal land of the Minangkabau in northern Sumatra, a long drum hangs from the sturdy rafters in a structure of its own. It is used only to call the faithful to prayer from far across the valley.

The rhythm of the drum is like a mirror of itself. Imagine a spiral winding toward a center point, then spinning and expanding to become a circle as wide as where it began. Imagine a ball bearing on this spiral, and each time it comes around it triggers the drum to be sounded.

As the spiral grows ever smaller
Drumbeat beating quickens,
tempo speeding
faster,
fast
rumbles like thunder,
then,
drum beat
tempo slowing
measurably slower
easy, leisurely slow and stop

My ball bearing enters at the bottom, going around on the spiral in a clockwise direction at first until it reaches the center. But once through the center the referent changes as you travel toward the nearest opening in a now-counterclockwise spiral although you are still going the same direction. This is a metaphor for moving from the third dimension to the next.

What a wonderful call to prayer.

Spirit Guides

The Banaue Blanket

I ARRIVED IN THE SMALL VILLAGE OF BANAUE in the Philippines near sunset and didn't have a room for the night. The rice terraces were stunning, and the light angle was perfect for photos.

(Once I had decided to be a photographer, the camera became ruler. Eventually I had to give it up; it is not possible for me to actively participate and record at the same time. Now the camera is for someone else to play with. Except the camera that keeps running in my mind.)

That day the camera still had the power to pull my stiff, hungry body back up the hill. The higher I walked along the road, the more expansive the view. The discomfort of the bus ride, the hunger from a day without a meal, the worry about finding a room for the night—all faded away. I followed my lens into dusk.

I was coming back down the hill toward the village when a woman from a family living alongside the road asked if I needed a room. Her family was more than happy to move out so that they could earn some extra pesos. The price? She charged per person; since I was alone, the room with the big bed was half price.

The room had corner windows, with rice terraces wrapped around either side. I could hear the water trickle along its designated paths, different streams on both sides.

At night from my bed I could see fireflies in a tree out one window blinking in unison—the whole tree at once—and out the other window another tree with fireflies blinking in unison but in a different rhythm. Trees turned into syncopated neon.

When I returned to my room the next day, the family asked if I were willing to move to their other room so that a traveling couple could come and stay. The other room was claustrophobic, with no windows. I couldn't breathe in there. Instead, I offered to look for another place. That would not be an option. Well, at least I could pay for the room I was in as if I were two people so they wouldn't lose money.

Stars When the Sun Shines

They wouldn't hear of it. They were embarrassed that they had asked me to move and pleased that I loved their room so much. They begged me to stay for as long as I wished. And that humble home in the rice terraces transformed itself into a temple.

What mind designed these mazes?
Growing on this steep incline
Taming water with terraces?
Who drew this amazing plan?

It would have insulted them if I had left the next day or even the following day. And so the money they could have made was cut in half for all that time.

They wouldn't accept a tip on the day I was leaving, searching my room as I was checking out so that nothing was forgotten; bringing back to me what I did "forget."

I noticed a blanket woven in the local pattern in bold black and red. She had woven it herself. It was for sale.

"How much you want for this?" I asked. "It's real nice."

The rules of bargaining in the Philippines are that if the seller is forced into setting a price, she sets it ridiculously high for a foreigner to start bargaining. The foreigner feigns a heart attack and cuts the price in half. Then they haggle until they come to a balance point, which is about twice the value that the locals pay.

"That will cost you. . . ." She said something in Tagalog that translated as "ridiculous price." I am shocked. I would never pay that much for a blanket and insisted she take 20 percent off. Sold. And the family was paid all the money they would have made and more, and face was maintained.

The Quiet of Lampang

Where the table-flat rice fields of Thailand touch the teak-covered northern mountains sleeps the provincial capital village of Lampang. The lazy Mae Wang River meanders through the heart of town, an artery in the Thai water-transport system that once brought many a small boat here. For a few decades Lampang was near the terminus of the railway. Whether they came by water or rail, passengers would disembark here, rest in the idyllic quiet, and then continue on to Chiang Mai on horse or elephant.

The paved highway bypassed the town. Time, as measured by change, slowed. Lampang remains the only city in all of Thailand where townspeople are still conveyed to and from the daily market in horse-drawn carriages. It's a little like time travel.

The quiet of Lampang is not apparent on the day I arrive. I have chanced upon a festival. Giant papier-mâché elephants with raised trunks form an arch over the main street. Women dressed in bright pastel handwoven silk blouses and in sarongs embroidered with shimmering gold thread parade beneath umbrellas or the traditional Thai lampshade hats. A few younger women in front carry banners with the names of the nearby hamlets they represent, shy majorettes in formal gowns. Others hold alms bowls containing small pagodas of tightly arranged flowers.

Men wearing the starched new dark indigo clothes of rice farmers with checkered scarves wrapped around their waists march by in ragtag file. Some carry tree branches with five-hundred-baht notes attached as leaves for gifts to the monastery. It is, naturally, a Buddhist festival. Floats on pickup trucks and palanquins carried on the shoulders of men flow by. A few have moving puppets that perform farm tasks in miniature: weaving, plowing, harvesting. Floats are decorated with leaves and flower sprigs, plastics and paper.

The parade snakes through the town to the sound of gongs, cymbals, hand drums, and long drums the size of cannons. Country flutes and Thai oboes play exotic wavering folk tunes, the equivalent in sound to the heat waves that rise from the pavement. Dancers— usually older men and women—raise their arms, twist their hands, and strut-dance back and forth across the street.

At the tail end of the parade fifty people using thick rope pull the largest float of them all. Riding on it is a bare-chested man, his face fiercely painted and his broad-blade scimitar drawn. A monk meditates on the highest level, his face hidden behind a fan. The fan shields him from the tempting sight of the virginal princess who sits opposite him but lower. On a silver tray she offers him a green, spherical watermelon.

The parade passes, but the crowd waits; word has reached us that a real princess of the Thai royal family will soon be coming. They wave their Thai flags and wait for an hour without becoming restive and are well rewarded when she rides by in her gold and white horse-drawn carriage.

On the morning of the second day of the festival I visit a Burmese-style temple, Wat Sri Choom, for a quiet moment out of the sun. The buildings are a flourish of carved wood. Frills and flowers surround the structure, crawl along the columns, and decorate the many-tiered towers with a filigree of cut tin for edging on the roofs. The temple grounds are as silent as the pool of still water behind the main chapel, where I sit in the shade.

"You!" A young monk is speaking to me. "There!" He directs me to a stairway and encourages me, with his hands waving, to enter the door at the top. Inside are the private quarters of the Venerable Kata Punno.

The old monk sits half reclined on his chair and footstool, surrounded by books in Burmese, Thai, and English: a tattered *Popular Science* magazine, assorted and incomplete sets of encyclopedias, a book by Asimov, a dictionary for Pali (an ancient sacred written language), stories of World War II . . .

He invites me to the chair beside him. "I am ninety-six years old. What I write I cannot read. What you say I cannot hear." He reaches for a hearing aid. "It helps only a little. Each day I hear less. I don't know why I still *live,*" and he laughs at his failings as if it were the grandest joke.

"We think when we are young that we are permanent. But everything changes."

I know what you are talking about, I think to myself.

"Everything changes. It is not something to worry about. According to Buddha, life is only life. Life isn't you. Life isn't me. Life is no one else. It is egoless. Without a core.

"We take life way too seriously. This mundane world is a world of half-truths. Everything will pass. You will pass. Even I will pass . . . someday. I am sure it will happen someday." Again the laugh. "Can you expect something permanent to come from something impermanent? Rid yourself of desire, and you will rid yourself of disappointment."

"And rid yourself of enjoyment, too, don't you think? Without desire, what would be the reason for doing anything?" I ask.

"I can't hear you," he says and reaches for a tablet and a pen. "Here, write down your question. Rather large, please, so I can read."

I do so.

"Without desire, what would be the reason for doing anything?"

He takes the tablet, read, then looks up at me. "Without desire? Who has no desire? Here at my age I am finally getting rid of a few, maybe. It takes a great deal of practice just to diminish desire. *Enjoy your problems. That is what they are for.*"

I leave him and return to town, where I come across another parade even bigger than the one yesterday. As I follow it through the streets I become aware of the contrast of colors and sounds of the crowd around me. Despite what the old ascetic monk might like to think, the world around me is anything but mundane.

The parade leads me to Wat Phra Keo Don Tau. When I arrive I see rows of women wearing long pointed brass fingernails. With their formal silk sarongs snug against their mango-shaped hips, they dance in unison: slow, subtle, sensuous movements to the sound of gongs, drums, oboe, and flute. Often three groups of dancers share the temple field, with three melodies being played at the same time and vying for attention with volume. Meanwhile another "tune" blares over a loudspeaker nearby, and the thudding drums of an arriving group at the end of the parade add to the cacophony.

This unit of young men, hand drums three feet long strapped around their necks, blasts all other sounds into the background. One of them grips the strap of his heavy drum in his teeth and climbs a pole made from four drums stacked one upon the next and held at the bottom by his fellows. He plays his drum, then clangs his cymbals while he dances on the top of a highest drumhead. Triumphant!

The flat open ground inside the outer walls of the temple fills with people in their finest new clothes pressing ever tighter together on the grass and gravel only a few feet from the dancers. Smiles. Excitement. They dance into the night.

The following day, the festival is over. I ride past the temple grounds, the site of yesterday's celebration. A cloud of dust and smoke hovers over the trashed field. There is sadness, a silence where only a day before there had been so much joy and life.

I stop over to say good-bye to the old monk; I am moving on. He invites me in for a short while. "Would you like a glass of water?" I bow and accept his offer, to be polite, although I feel no need. I take a sip. Tepid.

I tell him about the great festival that had just finished and how sad the place looked now that it is empty.

"Gautama Buddha listed five enemies of man: those who don't love you, robbers, fire, water, and the government," he tells me. "These things work against our desires. *If you have nothing, you want things. If you have them, you lose them or you worry about losing them.* This is all *dukkha,* unsatisfactory conditions. If you meditate on *dukkha,* you will see the hopelessness of desires."

"I don't see how meditating on sadness will bring you happiness," I write large on his tablet.

"*No, no. Not happiness. Freedom.* Would you like some more water?"

I point out that my glass is still full for I haven't taken more than a sip. "Freedom," he continues, "the state of enlightenment, is like a temple hidden in the middle of a thick forest. It's always there. You just don't see it."

"So why not put some road signs up along the path?" I ask.

"Everyone comes from a different direction and must find their own path. They will find their own signs if they are looking."

"So why not at least thin the forest so you can see there is a temple to go to?"

"If you thin the trees, the temple wouldn't be in the middle of a forest. Would you like some more water?"

"Thank you. I have plenty yet."

"I see," says the monk. "Do you see? *You must first empty your glass before you can fill it.*"

A glass filled up cannot take any more.
To fill your glass you must drink something first.
So if there's ever something you are hoping for
First you have to give way to your thirst.

Stars When the Sun Shines

"The sun, he not walk across sky?" The whites of his eyes glow with curiosity from his dark brown face. Nujen, an *orang asli* (meaning "original inhabitant"), talks with a voice soft in volume, soft in feeling, too, like a slow-moving stream—a tone at home in the dim edge of the sphere of light surrounding our flickering campfire.

A few days earlier I obtained special permission to visit the *orang asli* from the Malaysian government department in Temerloh that handles the affairs of these people. I hired a taxi out of town, passed an abandoned gold mine, and left the main artery for ever-narrowing capillaries of asphalt, then onto a slender gravel road snaking through plantations, row upon row of oil-palm and rubber trees blinking by on both sides. Several times I had to get out of the taxi so that the driver could take it through deep puddles with all fenders intact. Eventually he refused to take me any farther. I arrived at the lake on foot, with my pack on my back.

People began to gather. A young mother suckled a baby at her breast. Beside her sat a much younger girl struggling to pry open a betel nut in preparation for chewing. I looked around at all the women with blood red mouths, then turned to the girl and in halting Malay asked if she at her very young age already thought betel nut was delicious. She shook her head in disgust. The betel nut wasn't for her; she was preparing it for her sister, and she pointed at the teenage mother with the baby. I turned to the mother and asked, "Delicious?"

She misunderstood my question, looked down at the baby busy at her breast, then back up at me. She nodded, beaming a pure, red smile, and said, "Yes. Very delicious."

At that moment I met her husband, my guide for the next day's journey across the lake. Nujen took me down to the shore and showed me his dugout canoe with the prow plowed into the mud. He and his friend had carved it out of a large tree trunk.

"Not so difficult," he told me. "Take two men only ten day."

Nujen told me that his younger brother had gone off to take a job. "He cutting down trees for Chinese company so he can buy many thing from Chinese store. Now he has motorbike he not paid for but must keep running so can go work with tree-cutting men. He work many day to pay for bike and gas just so he can go work. Cut down trees so can pay to work. No sense."

"That's progress," I said sardonically.

"That progress? I think it same like when we catch iguana," he said. "We have special way for hunt iguana. First, our dogs smell one and chase him up tree. Then we go to tree and walk around and around till iguana, he watching us up there all time, he turning to keep us in his eyes, he get dizzy and fall down. Bam! When he hit ground he feel more dizzier. Then fast, we grab it by neck, but careful. Teeth like knife. Then quick, we grab tail and swing it at head.

"Iguana, he see tail attack and he bite. Can't help it 'cause he afraid. He bite hard; he real afraid. Then tail feel pain and head get more afraid so he bite even harder and won't let go. You can wear that iguana around your neck all way home. It won't never let go.

"Some people same like iguana, biting own tail and feeling pain so afraid to let go that they, for sure, going to end up in some stew."

The next morning we waded into the muddy ruddy shallows, climbed into Nujen's dugout canoe, and, using poles, began wending our way along the shallow path through reeds growing as thick as hair from the lake floor.

Lake Bera is actually a wide spot in a tea-colored river; it is caused by the reverse flow set up by a natural bottleneck leading into the Pahang River. In some parts where the water fingers around islands and far into valleys, the lake stretches five miles across. During the wet season, it expands to twenty miles from north to south.

The main channel flows lazily through an archway of overhanging trees leading in turn to a labyrinth of landless screw-pine islands. Although Nujen had been out on the lake often and even recently, he repeatedly made cul-de-sac turns. Time and again we were enticed down promising but dead-end lanes that narrowed into spike-needle gauntlets. The thorn-tipped leaves of the screw pine ripped clothes and lacerated skin from both sides of the boat. Flies buzzed all around.

The day grew steamy on the swampy lake. I wrapped my head in a sarong for protection from the brutal equatorial sun. When we came to open water, the still, quicksilver surface mirrored a second sun. Then clouds gathered, and we glided on white billows until we came to a hut standing high above the water.

The hut made use of three thin living trees and a pole for a fourth stilt. To hide from the midday heat, we climbed up a rickety ladder made of sticks tied together with vines.

We were invited into the dark interior. After we had been there for a short while, a strong wind picked up, sending the hut swaying on its stilts. Nujen and our host were spooked. They began to burn a piece of bark and chant a phrase over and over until the wind stopped and the hut stabilized.

That was this afternoon. Tonight we camp on the shore beside the lake. Nujen and I sit with our backs to the cooking fire. Night on Lake Bera: The air smells of wet mushroom. The black water reflects the gems of heaven, and fireflies dance in between. The planet Venus is being chased by the canoe moon.

Nujen points at what he thinks is a shooting star. I tell him it isn't a star, or even a meteor. It is man-made, a satellite.

"Man can live up there?" Nujen asks me in Malay. He is astounded. I tell him about men landing on the moon. He has heard something about this.

"So it true, lah! Then maybe your people know where sun go at night?"

I am condescending to this naive primitive, like one would talk to a child. I explain that the sun doesn't really go anywhere. "We are on a spinning ball."

"The sun, he not walk across sky?"

Can't blame him for thinking the sun moves. We in the West still say the sun "goes down" and "rises," even though we know the sun doesn't really move around the earth. Don't we?

He considers this for a while. "So, same true about all star during day? They all go far away from sun? Are they all other side of ball?"

"The stars are all around the ball of earth," I laugh. "You can't see them during the day because the sunlight is too bright. But they are still there," I assure him, imparting wisdom like King Solomon.

He seems confused, so I decide to talk of something familiar to him. "Would you mind singing that chant again, the one you and your friend sang to the wind this afternoon?"

He looks at me as if I were crazy. "No can now. No wind now," he explains as if he were talking to a child.

"What difference does that make? Come on, you can chant it now."

"No wind spirit now, so how can I sing to her?" He is silent for a moment. Then, "Lord." He calls me Lord?! "Lord, where does wind come from?"

I give him the old junior high school science explanation with a lot of hand gestures to help him understand: "Well, you see, the sun heats the ground, and the ground heats the air that is next to it, and hot air rises the same way as smoke rises from our flame here. And then the cold air rushes in to fill the empty space."

"Yah, lah!" Nujen's eyes are wide with excitement. "The spirits push the wind so it rush into empty place."

"No spirits. Spirits aren't necessary here," I tell him.

"So why wind blow?"

"Simply because nature doesn't like empty spaces. Trust me. The air flows naturally."

"Because wind spirit push it," insists Nujen.

"Why do you see any need for spirits here?" I argue. "You can't see any spirits, can you?"

"Cannot see spirit. Same like . . ."

Like the stars when the sun shines.

With questions worthy of Socrates, he showed me that my belief in the natural laws of science and his belief in spirits both rested on belief. It all depends on what I choose to believe. *Can one choose what to believe?*

Hope is the backbone of things
That are longed for but rarely are seen,
The force that brings into being
All that you long for, all of your dreams.
—Hebrews 1:11 W.U.V. (Wayne's Unstandard Version)

Stars When the Sun Shines

Dying to Try

I CAME OUT OF THE JUNGLE just as the train for Singapore was pulling out of the Kuala Lipis station. Caught it on the trot just like in the pictures. I got a spot in the mail car sitting on the floor, my back against the edge of the open slide-away door, and watched the rain forest disappear into the distant twilight.

Twelve hours later the train arrived among skyscrapers in the prelight before dawn. A friend picked me up at the station and in his topless MGB drove me over the long suspension bridge describing in highway the limit of the city high above the ocean, orange road lamps flashing overhead like a strobe. Yin Yang.

Whoa!

I decided to call Mars, having just completed half my intended trip with lots of material to write about. I felt flush, even a little light-headed, as if I had been drinking, which I hadn't in the rain forest. I was about to have a beer after the call.

I was doing what I wanted to do: discovering places rarely visited by outsiders, taking photos to die for—although I never liked that expression—and writing whatever I wanted to write. I felt unable to stop; in fact, the pace was increasing.

I am like a bull pulling a cart. When I come to something that causes me to change directions, I need to pull two carts, the second one in the new direction, and the first going where it was heading before the turn. At a corner, instead of slowing down for this extra weight, I tend to add energy to my load to compensate for the added strain. When I straighten out once more, rather than easing up, I continue applying the hyped-up energy. Everything speeds up with every turn.

I had no idea how much I was using velocity to maintain my equilibrium. Eventually the cart had to tip over. Right then, in Singapore, I was going strong, walking in high corn as they say, in my stride in the middle of my eight-month adventure.

Mars was lonely. She asked me to come back home to her in Hawaii.

I missed her, too. "I'll be home in Honaunau in a few days."

Stars When the Sun Shines

We had moved to Hawaii a mere six months before my present trip. We moved mostly because Mars wanted to. It didn't matter to me where I wrote. In order to pay for the move I sold my wedding ring, our stereo, and our cream-colored 1947 Plymouth Super Deluxe with the chocolate bonnet. An antique now, the car was born the same year I was. It was pure street theater. And it was just passing through my life for a while. Time for change. When you live like we do, you don't hang on to possessions.

We moved into a coffee shack overlooking Kealakekua Bay. The name of the bay, we discovered, meant "Pathway of the Gods." In the weeds next to our home I discovered a 1947 Plymouth, the same model as the one we had lovingly left behind in California. A metaphor. We still have the memories.

......

On that trip I picked up a lot of wonderful stories and also something else. Fortunately, I got home before the malaria set in.

Malaria is a headache—a dog whistle you can hear, and you want to howl! It pierces your soul. It is unkind. No. Worse! Malaria is merciless. Grand inquisitors would drool to know its secrets.

Malaria begins with a chill, a flush of excitement, a rush of giddiness like my first bottle of cold beer after a hot day's work. Dainty dew forms on the brow, and soon perspiration drenches the armpits. There's dizziness. Your eyes won't focus; nausea grabs the back of your neck and hangs you in the air by a clamp at the base of your skull. There's a looseness of mind and of bowels, an overwhelming weakness that makes raising an arm to switch off a light as impossible as climbing Mount Everest on Rollerblades. You feel an I-want-my-mama depression growing darker by shades into why-was-I-born-at-all despondency. Eventually you struggle with unemotional, smoothly logical thoughts of suicide.

There is a blizzard raging inside you. You get the hippy-dippy shakes like Saint Vitus with his finger stuck in an electric socket. At the same time you feel as if red peppers are being rubbed into every pore of your skin. You get drenched. Streams form rivulets of sweat flowing along your skin like snakes, and an Amazon pours into the bedsheet sea. I recommend malaria only if you are dying to lose weight fast and can't stand the taste of arsenic.

I was hallucinating. My eyes closed tight trying not to slide off the merry-go-round that was spinning too fast. I remember the rain pounding on the corrugated roof roaring louder than a volcano and embracing me in a tight suffocating blanket that held my aching mind inside my skull.

The rain abruptly stops. Silence. In that vacuum the roof is sucked off the coffee shack and my mind shoots out over Kealakekua Bay. The visuals!

I awoke with a movie in my mind of a sixty-year-old Japanese man who was about to meet his nineteen-year-old picture bride, the beginning of the book *Hawaii Blue*.

My books aren't really fiction in the sense that I make up stories. I write about myself as a fictitious character, a persona who tends to be stupider than I pretend to be outside my writing. Other characters in my books are creations of my imagination, although I often use prototypes, usually a composite of a few people I have observed perhaps just in passing. These fictitious characters take on a life of their own and lead me to the story rather than it being written by me.

It is the old turning-the-ball-inside-out trick. You see, it can't be me that is writing the book because I am busy being inside the book. I figure it is the ego that is trapped in the book. Oh! Oh! I believe I just fell into a Möbius reality. Let us return to the old man's story.

The elderly Japanese man looks forward to explaining to his young picture bride what *aloha* means to him, a Japanese who grew up in Hawaii. It will be like teaching a child, he muses. Oh how sweet it will be, sharing a green-flash sunset with her.

The second part of the story takes place a few years later: Mr. Holy—the way he ironically pronounces his name, Hori—his mind racing, "I know what she's doing taking off her clothes in the light, standing between the lamp and the pulled window shade so that she can send her beautiful shape out to anyone who wishes to look.

"And they are looking. You can bet on that. I know men better than she does. Lots of men looking. I'm gonna take care of this problem right away. I put fluorescent light in her room. No shadow."

He is not capable of handling a problem directly.

"What is taking her so long? It doesn't take that long. Oh sure, she tells me she stops on her way back to the house to look at the beautiful stars. I am the one who showed her how to look at them. I'll bet she's looking at the stars, on her back she's looking. Probably getting a good view.

"Main t'ing, cool head. I'm gonna stop that right here and now. Tomorrow I'm gonna find out how much it will cost to get indoor plumbing."

I was using humor to handle my feelings of discomfort about my lack of control over my destiny. The malaria had knocked me back, hard. I had been a half step from death inside delirium. I refused to go get medical help. Mars ordered me to the car, crawl if I had to, so she could take me to the doctor. It took a shot in the butt to turn me around. I was supposed to go back for a booster but never did. Didn't have the money or the faith in doctors.

Circa 1989, on one of many return trips to Malacca to do research on a book about King Solomon's gold, an old Indian friend, Albert Dawson, took me out to his patio garden, where a shrub grew out of a large planter. He told me that when he was a child, his mother was so poor she sent him and his brother to live with a stranger out on the rubber plantation, where they both came down with malaria. They lay on a cement floor with only a sarong for a bed and a blanket. An ancient Tamil with white hair and the wrath of God on his brow commanded that they come outside and eat from this shrub.

Neither he nor his brother has ever had a relapse of malaria, which is unusual for this disease. Some would say impossible. He insisted I eat a few leaves. It was so bitter it flavored my food for days after. I have never had a single malarial relapse. So much for booster shots.

......

My books weren't selling. The money I was making from my travel writing did little more than pay for my travels. Hawaii was a rock; I couldn't seem to get my roots growing in it. I needed to write *Hawaii Blue* in order to find a way to feel that it was OK for me to live in paradise, if in fact it would ever be OK.

By the third part of the story the man I described as naively hopeful at sixty had turned into a very sad old man at eighty, married to a woman half his age, with a rebellious surfer son of twenty years. He was all alone, caught in despair. I wrote seeing life through his eyes, through his dry tears.

He stands, noose around his neck, on a thickly painted white wooden kitchen chair with a round back.

He notices an ugly spot of chipped paint exposing the dark blue enamel of a previous coat underneath. *Never repainted it,* he muses.

"Here, old man. I'll help you die. Get you out of your misery."

I guess that shows where my mind was heading at the time. Happiness had not been the result of my successes. And the space between magazine articles and books was becoming the same as the space between plays had been earlier in my life. Empty. I had been driven. My wagon tipped over.

Velocity in its absence kills equilibrium.

The story that started *Hawaii Blue* about the old Japanese man never made it into the book. I showed the piece only to Mars. Two weeks after I wrote it, one of the Japanese men I imagined as a prototype committed suicide precisely as I described, down to the chip of dark blue on a chair I am not sure I'd ever seen before. *What is going on?* What was the relationship of my words, my thoughts, to reality? Was I prescient? Was I somehow a cause? It spooked me.

I was sure I couldn't afford to deal with reality flippantly, playfully making it up. I decided from then on to stay clear of negative stories, negative thoughts. Let me say that another way: I intend to think positively, always.

It is worth noting that I started *Hawaii Blue* instead with a story of a car running over a prosthesis in the snow and snapping it off at the stump. An elderly German snaps his leg back on, gets up, waddles to his car, and drives off. The irony of this will soon become apparent.

I was hard on typewriters, and even the industrial-strength ones couldn't hold up under the brutal hours I would stand over them learning what the heck I wanted to say and then starting over and rewriting everything twenty or thirty or more times. What was the problem? As Hemingway answered: "The problem was getting the words right."

Hemmingway wrote while standing. I believe it was because of hemorrhoids. So did I, for different reasons. To keep my energy going I stood and even danced while I wrote. I pounded my energy down onto those keys, sometimes beating out a rhythm of my choosing. Someone suggested that I stood to write because if I sat down it would constrict my brain. I couldn't argue with her.

While I was in the middle of writing *Hawaii Blue,* my electric typewriter died. My third industrial-strength typewriter in four years. No typewriter! How can I write this book? My penmanship is so bad that my teacher Mrs. Cemenski once asked me if I could read my own writing. I told her that I most certainly could most of the time. "If you can find another person on the planet who can read this, you have yourself a secret code." Like the Navajo code talkers of WWII. I never was able to find that person.

Longhand was not an option. I killed typewriters. I needed to upgrade to a computer. This was in 1985, when the idea of the personal computer was fledgling.

The same day that my last typewriter was still smoking, Mars informed me that we had only two dollars left to our name. We'd done it again and spent all our money. Saving for the future doesn't make much sense when you are dying. Neither does health insurance. Nor are they needed if you are relying on chance.

"Hmm. Looks like one of us is going to have to get a job. I might as well. My writing isn't going anywhere. I'll start looking tomorrow."

"I already got a job at our friend Jack's health store. You keep writing." I love this woman.

So she went off to work, and I went into a stew for not being able to write, even though I had no writer's block. I yelled into the sky in my frustration: "I thought you wanted me to be a writer! You know, you aren't exactly participating in the process. The way the books are selling, we're looking at best-kept-secret status, thank you.

"Wait. It is probably my fault. It might be that I am no good. I asked to be able to write. The *being good* part has to be up to me. I just haven't delivered. This could be all ego talk, me as a writer. Maybe I should give up this manic obsession of mine. I'm going to need a computer to continue anyway. And with no money, no chance.

"We can make this real simple. I'll make you a deal," still talking to the ethers. "You give me a computer, and

I'll continue writing. If you don't, no problem. I'll go do something else. Sorry I ever bothered you about it in the first place." I said this bitterly. I figured I had quit writing. I had stopped doing the only thing that was bringing any meaning into my life at all. It was a real down time.

Mirror-gazing time. Didn't work. I'll try again tomorrow, and tomorrow and tomorrow.

I drove up to the shop seven miles from our coffee shack to pick up Mars after work. Jack Davis, bless his memory, the owner of the health store, asked me to come in to chat for a spell.

"I have had this store for seventeen years. It's a clean business and it's been good to me, but now I want to do something with my days other than retail. Wayne, would you like to buy this store?"

He surprised me. I answered without thinking, or in other words, honestly: "Not at all. But why are you asking me? You got something against women? Why don't you ask Mars? She's the one working for you."

"You're right." I had spoken the truth, and he admitted his bias graciously. My truth wasn't usually accepted so well by others.

"OK, Mars. Do you want to buy the store?"

"Sure, I'd like to," as if her wildest dream were to come true.

"In that case, I also would love to buy your store, Jack, with all my heart. Mars usually starts things, and I get excited about them later. And then I usually overdo it," I added, remembering how I entered theater, began to travel, and so on.

"Great. I can't think of two people who would be better for our customers. Now, we are talking—he named a figure in the thousands—for the stock on hand, and I'd say another number in the thousands for the name that has been built up. I believe it is a very reasonable price. How much can you give me down?"

I smiled. "I'll give you half of all the money I have."

"Can't ask for more than that and be fair."

So I pulled a dollar out of my wallet and handed it to him. He looked down, puzzled. He didn't believe I was telling the truth. I have this way about me that textures truth into appearing as fiction. But when he looked at Mars, he accepted it as fact. For one dollar down, we bought the store.

And with the health store came my first computer, on which I wrote *Hawaii Blue*.

All you have to do is ask.

The book didn't sell well to locals, who were not curious about an island they had always known, and it hadn't any appeal to tourists who were looking for hula girls and palm trees. Of course, we had no budget for advertising. My experience with a publisher before made me spurn any idea of writing to someone else's template. In fact, considering our financial situation, I suggested we not publish the book at all, but Mars insisted. If I was going to do what I wanted in writing the book, she would get to do what she wanted in publishing it. I could not refuse.

About a year and a half after we "purchased" the place, the local economy went into a tailspin and the health store started losing money. After falling in love with Hawaii, it was hard to think of leaving, but we needed the money, so I returned to teaching in Tokyo. I figured I had been given the sign I had asked for and been kicked off the island. Mars joined me a month later after I had found an apartment and a job. We hired a manager for the store and sent money back to keep him happy and to pay off what we still owed, but the manager did little to keep the doors open. Nor did the next one. Eventually, the doors had to be closed.

I went back to Tokyo in February 1988 after a ten-year absence. On one of my first nights back, I returned to the *nomiya* hole-in-the-wall where I had spent so much time a decade ago. The entrance was down a long narrow stairway into the basement bar. I arrived in the afternoon. A young man in an apron seemed startled to see a foreigner. I was confused. Perhaps I wasn't in the right place. In bad Japanese, for I had forgotten much, I said that I had often come to this bar years earlier.

Machan, the stranger, looked at me and said, "Wayne?" He had started working there seven years after I left Japan, and yet he knew my name.

I was able to insinuate myself and Mars back into the university where we had quit so abruptly years earlier.

Dying to Try

Nothing had changed. Initially I was without a computer, so I was again not writing. Nothing had changed. All those years of travel, all those lessons I had written about, and yet nothing had changed.

Except I couldn't go back into Kyōgen. My legs were now older, and I was even less patient with training. I had lived on my own too long for that to be possible. I tried. It didn't work. I was not going to go any further in the study, and frankly, modern Japan was now completely removed from its roots. Zen seemed like a party trick.

Tokyo was once again an absurd game. How could I complain? I had the prestige of being a well-paid professor as well as having been a Noh actor.

I wrote a satire on travel and Tokyo, called "Iron Tourist in Tokyo," that was published in an airline magazine and a Tokyo Sunday magazine. In it I laid out a plan to see everything of "significance" in the city in a single day, eat a variety of Japanese food, and travel on every conceivable means of public transportation. It was exactly the type of travel I had never wished to do again unless it was a kind of a pinball game.

It was a wonderful day, with absurdities and meaningless miracles showing up constantly through the piece. I even went to play *pachinko* and watched as rows of ball bearings poured into my basket, which I took to the counter and traded in for cigarette coupons, which I then took down the alley to cash in for money. Gambling outwardly in Japan is illegal. Form is everything. The result: the day of absurd travel turned out to be entirely free. It seemed to point out to me that I wasn't.

Everything I had learned while traveling around the world seemed meaningless in the everyday machine of Tokyo. I was repeating daily what I had repeated daily a decade earlier. I felt like Sisyphus, condemned to the meaningless task of rolling a boulder up the mountain slope only to have it roll back to the bottom when he nears the top. He is cursed to go back down and begin the task again.

Letting Go with Effort

ON MANY VACATIONS WE TOOK during these years in Tokyo, we would go as far away from the city as we could. We found a remote island called Koh Phangan in the middle of the Gulf of Thailand that had yet to be discovered by the masses of itinerant world travelers with noses in their guidebooks helping them get away from their parents. This became my retreat. I lived in Tokyo waiting for my time away from it. Tokyo Cowboy Wayne hid the hermit inside me behind a clown facade.

I had put on weight again—getting back to our apartment after work around midnight for my presleep pizza and beer. In Thailand this weight increase caused the string that was holding up my hammock to break. I fell heels over head down to the hard sand. My head had wedged between two tree roots, with my butt sticking up in the air. Mars had to pry me from this awkward position. She was laughing. It was embarrassing.

The fall bruised my ribs. It was very funny, and it hurt quite a bit when I laughed. Don't want sympathy for a slapstick performance. The trick is to get up quickly and pretend it didn't happen.

Pretending was difficult. I couldn't get rid of the pain. This started slowly but increased over the years. I kept thinking I could twist out the kink, but with no luck. I could take only fifty steps at a time before I had to stop and wait minutes for the ache in my left leg to subside. After a couple of years it became impossible to continue teaching because of the walks to and from train stations. We left Japan after six long years and moved to our private beach in Thailand.

We had plenty of money at that time, and finally again our dream come true: no schedule. Mars studied Thai. I was writing what I intended to be my last book, *Malacca Gold,* while supine in a hammock next to a sunset beach with a laptop on top of my lap.

I remembered the lightning that struck the island just off of Malacca when I was with Father Sir Lancelot. So later when I came across a story of a Javanese princess and a lost treasure of a hundred tons of gold buried down a well shaft, I did some research. I learned that such a large cache of gold would cause lightning to strike even that small iron-red island. When I learned that the name of a local mountain was Ophir, the fabled land from where King Solomon received his tons of gold, I developed the story for my novel, *Malacca Gold*.

In part of the book I visualized a character called Lucky Lim, an illiterate Chinese coolie who somehow mysteriously became very rich in 1920 when the rubber prices had bottomed out. At the end of his life he bought a very expensive grave site because of its extraordinary feng shui. I wrote of how punters would go sit by the grave and dream up their lucky lottery number.

On one of my many visits to Malacca, I asked Humphrey Ball, who had become my Old Man of Malacca, for he knew the city as well as any Englishman could, if he thought the story of Lucky Lim sounded at all plausible culturally.

"You are talking about my good friend Tun Tan San Shwei."

"No," I corrected him. "I'm talking about a character I made up."

"Come. I shall show you the grave."

We climbed the gentle stairs on the walkway to the top of Malacca's highest hill. When we reached the omega-shaped grave, Humphrey explained that it was considered lucky because it was lined up with the mountain called Ophir.

"Aren't all two object in line with each other? It is only significant if there is a third point," I observed. I was sitting on one of the benches at the leg of the grave. I turned away from the mountain and found myself looking straight through the only two skyscrapers in downtown Malacca as if they were uprights and my eyes were the path of a football going through the center of the goalposts. I followed the path across the orange roof tiles of two-story shop-homes all the way to the village on the coast and beyond to the island of lightning. My book wasn't fiction. *What is going on?*

The problem: the Chinese secret-society gang known locally as the Four Holes and internationally as the 14K have a torture of a thousand cuts that prolongs the agony of death until you give them a secret. Knowing where a hundred tons of King Solomon's gold is hidden became an uncomfortable secret to have. So I wrote the book telling everyone exactly where the gold is hidden but using an unreliable narrator so that the story sounds like a tall tale. It is ironic to know where there are a hundred tons of gold while you're out of money. Yet I couldn't think of any good that would come from my going to get it.

For exorcise, for exercise I rode my bicycle using mostly my right leg along water-buffalo trails through coconut fields all around the island of Koh Phangan, trying my best to get lost. It wasn't possible on the small island. Downhill was always toward the ocean, and the coast always led me home.

Stars When the Sun Shines

I tried swimming at warm dawn before the heat of the day but could only manage winged backstrokes, both arms pulling me at once and bulleting my head through mercury waters, dragging my tired leg behind me. The water copied the clusters of clouds, and I flew in between. I could do this for miles in tepid water the same temperature as the air.

The sun is rising over coconut palm. A school of silver fish rainbows over and around my head. Ah! Beauty. What more could I want? Enough. This would be an excellent moment to die. Instead, my leg hurts, and it's picking up hertz. I turn and stroke home backward, dragging my left leg behind.

......

After four years living on a white sand beach in Thailand, Mars and I traveled to the Midwest, U.S.A., for my folks' sixtieth anniversary. On the way back we stopped over on Hawaii Island. I was body surfing badly at Hapuna Beach and came to shore coughing.

A woman approached me at water's edge. "Excuse me. Are you Wayne Stier, author of *Hawaii Blue?*"

"You read *Hawaii Blue?*" I had met very few people up to then who admitted they had.

She had loved it. It was her all-time favorite book. I nearly fainted. Does she need to get a life or what? She said I had captured the elusive *aloha* spirit that pervades the island but is often invisible and hard to grasp. At that moment she let the *aloha* flow back over me, over us. To our mutual surprise, Mars and I decided that we would move back home to Hawaii.

We had ridden the economic elevator up to dizzying heights. There were days we made a thousand dollars doing nothing. We rode the elevator back down just as quickly and managed to get off about where we got on. That's what you get for doing nothing. Money became a meaningless metaphor. It is, however, a handy way to interface with those who still believe in it.

Hawaii had become extremely expensive in the ten years we had been away. We found an old friend who was in the middle of a divorce who had converted a detached laundry room into a detached bedroom, which he rented out to us while we looked for a place to live.

Kathy, the former wife of his gardener—was anyone but us married to their first partner anymore?—now rented the coffee shack where I had written *Hawaii Blue*. (After all that travel, after ten years away from Hawaii, we had landed back on Painted Church Road a mere two hundred yards from our former home.) She had found a copy of *Hawaii Blue* at a yard sale for a dollar and loved it. She wondered if I would mind autographing her copy. I was honored.

That wasn't to be a sale, and we were naturally in need of money, but Kathy brought over a friend who had a bed-and-breakfast. Friend Nita bought three of my books and offered to sell me a wood-burning stove she didn't need because her B&B was at a lower elevation than she had anticipated. She sold it to us for what it had cost to ship the heavy cast-iron stove, a savings equivalent to the profits of about a thousand books. Now all I needed was a place to put the woodstove.

We magically found a sylvan treasure, a piece of land upslope from the place where the Polynesians first touched Hawaiian lava. We found it under the star Arcturus twenty-five years after I asked for a sign: Wayne Stier, Wagon Star, Star of Gladness. Yes, I belong in paradise. Everyone does. Our acre is covered with big four-hundred-year-old ohia trees that blossom with red lehua flowers like the Queen of Hearts' garden in *Alice in Wonderland*. A driveway with curves that remind me of a Japanese garden led to an existing structure open on two sides, with no floor and a tin corrugated roof with only a few holes on the north side. Open rafters. It had been a potting shed for a nursery. How could we resist?

It already had a loft held up by ten ohia trees. Whoever did this work of art, thank you. *Mahalo.* It makes our home a one-of-a-kind wonder.

I had played around with designing a house once in Bali, where a Javanese architect staying in the next bungalow taught me some basics. I designed our house for us with open rooms, with lots of windows. Soon we had a plywood floor laid, some walls tilted into place, and a metal roof overhead in our add-on kitchen-and-bedroom section. We moved in and camped with

Letting Go with Effort

flapping plastic. In a while electricity and plumbing moved in with us, a sliding window, a plethora of windows bought at a rummage sale, and even windowed French doors that open up to the world out front. Furniture?

I had very little training as a carpenter. In fact, it had only been one day when I was fifteen. I was hired to help roof a barn, and, too afraid of letting people know of my fear of heights, I went with the crew.

When they needed a volunteer to hand up the planks, I was ready and eager to stay on the ground. Young, energetic. Soon they had "all the wood we need up here for a spell, boy."

Along comes the boss's lovely daughter, my age. Cute as can be. My gosh. Look at them dimples. We got to talking. It was Saturday. What you doing tonight?

"Board!" someone above was yelling. *"Board?"*

"Bored? Heck no, I'm having a great time."

Yet despite my training in carpentry, Mars and I were able to build our house almost entirely by ourselves. Called my dad after we finished. He asked me if the roof was still on. He laughed. He knew me.

"Still on and no leaks, Dad. Go figure." Dad passed on before he could visit. When Mom came and saw our house, she joked, "If your father had seen what you built, the shock would have given him a heart attack." He would have had ample reason to be shocked. When we were kids, whenever dad needed a screwdriver, my brother would be right there ready to hand it to him

Stars When the Sun Shines

before he even knew what he needed. Me, I was always daydreaming. He would tell me to fetch the screwdriver, and I would hurry right back with pliers.

Mars helped hold an end of the two-by-four while I secured the other end. The use of a clamp to replace her may have saved our marriage. We decided to work together separately. She did as much as I. She did almost all the painting. I am grateful to those who came to our rescue when we were in extreme need during construction. Most of the time, help arrived just when we were desperate. I rarely had to ask.

When I wanted advice, I would go to the hardware store and talk story. I validated the skill of a lot of laborers with my ignorance. Interesting that what I knew helped less than what I didn't know in making new friends.

"Seems it's time for plan B again," I said one day to Mary, a clerk at the hardware store.

Mary responded, "Wayne, you do not have a plan. You have a hypothesis." That is how glowingly my ignorance was showing. Yet does anyone really have a plan? Really? It felt comforting that someone understood where I was coming from. Life is a hypothesis.

I was enjoying myself so much that Mary teasingly asked if I might want to become a contractor after this. I told her no. I was having the time of my life building my own home to my eccentric design, but if I were doing it for money, I'd be bitter. I think the same thing had become true for writing. That is why I had quit.

We are on catchments—no bills for water when we are blessed with rain. When we came here the land was in a nine-year drought. People complained as a hobby. I told them not to worry. The rain would come once my gutters were on. Be a waste until then. When they complained again, I noted that none of them had come over to install my gutters for me. It rained the day the gutters were ready for water.

The pain in my back and left leg was getting worse. In respect for the sacred quiet of where I live, the rush of winds and the song of birds, I decided against using power tools. Conveniently, this gave me a lot longer to realize when I was making a mistake. And the physical labor helped me explain some of my pain at the end of the day. I could somehow ignore it if I could find another good reason to hurt. Sore muscles. Hard work. I've been there before.

My eyes became expert at finding the exact length of two-by-four for my need so I could avoid yet another saw cut with my tired body. Need something fifteen and seven-eighths inches long? I would miraculously find exactly that. It happened many times.

If I came to a problem I couldn't solve, I would sleep on it. The next morning I would have the solution. Once I woke with a solution, but when I went to work that day, to my surprise I found myself doing something else first. Later that day, I came to the conclusion that my solution wouldn't have worked.

Sometimes what I did was plain stupid. There is a story of a man in a hurry who wanted to know the fastest way to become an Alaskan. He was told he would have to chug down a fifth of whiskey, wrestle a grizzly, and make love to an old woman. He finished the fifth in a few gulps and then, rubbing his hands, headed out to the woods. Ten days later he came back all cut up with his clothes torn to shreds.

One day I came off the ladder realizing that what I had been doing the last few hours had been utterly futile. I looked at Mars and shook my head. "Where's that old lady you want me to wrestle?"

We had solar panels installed and are free forever from electric bills. It helps that we are also free from the microwave, the dishwasher, the clothes dryer, and the TV. We moved into our house with a floor in two months. Woodstove was burning and cozy by the time it got cold.

A friend saw the trees in my house and brought over some slabs of monkey pod that make wonderful natural shelving to go with the ambient rustic decor. One of the pieces, however, was an awkward five inches wide and twenty-five inches high at the peak of a triangle. It could not be a shelf. What am I going to do with this?

Carried it down to my shed to store it when I came across a half inch rounded chisel on my workbench. Before building the house I bought tools at yard sales.

Didn't have a clue what many of them were for. Didn't remember buying a chisel, but might have, I suppose.

I picked it up and, using a regular steel hammer, hit my knuckle. That smarts. The next time, I watched the hammer and chisel carefully and missed the wood. The next stroke only nicked the wood. The next stuck the blade. I turned the wood around, and a chip went flying across the carport. And again. Zoom. Again. This is fun.

Two weeks later I had finished a piece called *Ready or Not*. I had unknowingly carved the pain in my leg into the contorted figure of a person. I had planned to carve myself a crying Buddha who covers his face from the pain of the world. Too much even for Buddha. I identified. I intended to have the figure hiding from reality.

However, it was the first hand I had ever carved. Instead of a thumb and four fingers I carved four lines between the fingers, creating one digit too many. I needed to cut a finger out, and in doing so the figure now peeks out from his cocoon, symbolizing that first moment of risk, the moment one begins to move away from fear. *Ready or Not*. The figure changed from being one of abject despair into one of hope. By an apparent mistake. Or was it?

It was a very good carving for a first piece. Probably beginner's luck. I began a second piece immediately, finished it quickly, and at once started a third. I didn't want to be bothered to sign them. As soon as one piece was finished, I was hungry to start another. Like writing, like theater, like travel.

Friends began to bring koa, mango, ebony. I was given a wide selection of chisels. Six months after I began my first piece, I discovered that the friend who had given me the monkey pod for *Ready or Not* had planted that chisel on my workbench. How did he know?

Carving wood requires one to work in opposites. Hold the hammer in the right hand loosely and it will fly across the carport. Hold the wrist tight; the strength of the stroke is diminished. It has to be loose like when you are playing bongos. On the other hand, hold the chisel tight and your hand absorbs the blow instead of the wood. Hold your wrist limp and you cannot guide the chisel with precision. After many trials this becomes a thoughtless natural process. Success with a blow is a gateway for learning. So in fact is failure, but it isn't as evident.

Another thing I noticed while chiseling: the pain in my leg was not as noticeable as the pain in my hand. I missed a lot. I carved long hours and threw out my arm. This provided me with another reason for pain away from the need to worry.

Cancer? Was this the final call? As long as I can stay away from the hospital.

I would get tired, stubbornly keep going, and hurt myself more. If a knife was used in the process, it always found a way into my flesh. The need to concentrate was apparent. Whenever I was able to get inside the wood, time disappeared and with it pain.

The wood draws me, takes me on a ride. You go with the ride that is offered. I look soft-focus at the grain until an image appears. As did the masters of old before me, I merely carve away what doesn't belong. It wasn't like I really actually carved anything from what I made up. I was only copying what I imagined was in the wood.

A mosquito bites me. I feel pain in my foot. How long have I been being bitten and not known it, had pain and not felt it?

People often ask me how long does it take to do a carving. I answer truthfully that it takes no time at all. The Arabs have an expression: *Allah does not subtract from man's allotted time the hours spent fishing.*

The truth is that time doesn't exist unless you are doing what you don't want to do. Or unless you are trying to relate to those who are on time.

"I have no watch, but I have all the time in the world."

I carved a doorstop in the form of a foot and called it *Door to Door Salesman.* That was probably inspired by the summer of '67, when Mars and I met while selling books door-to-door. I carved mermaids and unapproachable maidens. I sculpted a Magic Mountain and magicians, a *"Double Header"* with heads at both ends, and two hands on a plaque reaching out, ready to receive. I carved a mask of a *Laughing Buddha* in the style of that Noh mask I had not been allowed to touch.

I was honored to be selected for a one-man show at the Wailoa Center garden gallery in Hilo. The recognition produced no sales. It was hard to find room for all the pieces after the show. I had run out of rooms for all my carvings. I didn't really try to sell. I am an artist, not a merchant. I also was afraid of what happens to the honesty of my art when I sell. I am an artist, not a merchant—maybe only because I haven't sold.

My largest piece—*Lilith and Adam,* the couple entwined in making love—is carved from a burl that grew next to a flame koa, a rich hardwood with tiger's-eye in the grain. However, parts of the wood in this piece were so loose they could not be chiseled or even rasped. I could only use a sharp blade, and finally medium-grain sandpaper, to form the figure. Consequently, the sanding of this piece took weeks, perhaps months. I have no way of knowing.

Each day I would go down to the carport, grab a piece of sandpaper, and continue. I didn't know where I went those days.

I know now: tMpL n 4st.

One day I found myself stroking the wood with no sandpaper in my hand. I was startled. I am finished with this now.

It was getting impossible for me to stand up and harder to concentrate on carving. Eventually I quit carving just as I had quit football, acting, travel, and writing.

Letting Go with Effort

I'm better with my writer's hat
Than I am when I sculpt
Yet when the chisel I am at
My sculpting I exalt.
Compared to when I try to act
Yet acting catapults
Above my writing, that's a fact.
My mind is on a Möbius route.

Where's that old woman you want me to wrestle?
I give up!

Over Sole

....

MY FOOT WAS FLOPPING DOWN LIKE A CLOWN'S. "What's the matter? Tie your shoe too tight this morning?" I bless that woman and wish her abundant karma until she can receive the blessing. Doctors couldn't find any reason for the flop. They were certain I had diabetes, but the test results didn't confirm their assumption. Their conclusion: test again. In the meantime they wanted to treat only the symptom of pain, with drugs from their patrons, the drug companies. I refused to live my life on pills.

But the pain was waking me at night. I would lie awake waiting to get up at three in the morning in order to go to our outdoor shower in the mountain Hawaiian winter, forcing myself to stand under full-on cold water to get my mind somewhere other than the pain if even for a moment. It worked. That cold water grabbed my attention. As soon as I became the least bit comfortable, however, the aching always returned.

I discovered that pain could be divided into three parts. Yesterday's pain has already been paid for. I could let that go. To assume there would be pain tomorrow meant I had given up hope. I couldn't afford the burden of hopelessness. I hadn't the energy left to cope with despair. Take away yesterday and tomorrow, and that left me with the pain of the moment.

I concentrate on now; the pain disappears. My ego disappears.

Wayne starts screaming his demand to exist, searches frantically for pain. He opens the door and pain rushes back in, bringing yesterday and tomorrow and tomorrow with it.

Again with effort born of need I relax into now. Feels good. Ego on loudspeaker: *"Are you feeling any pain, Wayne? Anywhere?* Oh. That's too bad. You poor thing." I slip back into the shell of my ball bearing as the pain pours in, making my outer edges solid. And I keep bouncing from bumper to bumper and back in this pinball game.

I decided enough was enough. Once and for all I would stretch out this kink that was taking over my life. I lay on my back with my arms spread to each side, and from my hips I crossed over my left leg to touch my right hand. It resisted. I insisted. I twisted my leg severely. The pain would not defeat me. Snap.

Stars When the Sun Shines

All blood stopped flowing to my foot. In a few days gangrene set in. It took several doctors to admit they didn't know what was happening. I was sent to Queens Hospital, Honolulu, where it was discovered I had a blood clot in my stomach from the hammock fall.

Fourteen years of pain, a blood clot. It could have killed me instead. But it didn't. Thank God?

The blood clot occurred because an artery had collapsed, having been weakened by the radiation I was given after my cancer operation thirty years before. The doctors, in a primitive attempt to cure my physical body, had weakened the walls of my arteries with radiation. No one ever informed me of this danger. Did they know? The artery collapsed when I fell from the hammock because I was fat, causing the stoppage of blood and all that pain. It hadn't been the cancer that was the worry all this time; it was the cure that caused the ultimate problem.

Now I had to return to the hospital, the place I feared more than the grave. I had no room for the luxury of fear. My life was turning into a nightmare. I took a deep breath.

I have reasons to believe that my life is magical.
Look at what has happened, the blessings, the miracles.
I'll pay for all the good times if it comes to that.
I will not become a victim by cursing my fate.
That means the doctors can't be villains.
I am captain of my destiny. I am willing.

Over Sole

I was given a double bypass to get blood flowing back into my legs. When I woke up after the operation, the pain was gone. *What follows may be difficult to relate.*

I discovered that I had accepted the pain as part of my person. Pain was my karma—or, in the parlance of the American Midwest, my *comeuppance*—for having spent so much of my life having a great time. I had been making my life an epic tragedy when I wasn't making it a cosmic joke. My ego had been busy playing both sides.

Now the pain is gone. I'd been leaning into it for so long, and now, stumbling forward, I fall on my face in warm snow. I'm free. Stars when the sun shines. The ball bearing turns inside out, and I am no longer trapped inside. I look back at who I was and smile like the memory of the Buddha whose expression I had imitated but a moment ago. Good judgment comes from experience. Experience comes from bad judgment.

Love comes from no judgment.

I have many reasons to be wise, but nothing to be proud of except that I made my mistakes on purpose. They were my doing. Things didn't just happen to me.

I'm sorry to me
& all
I forgive me
& all
I love me
& all
Thank you to me
& all

Stars When the Sun Shines

My cup overflows. I love me. Feels awkward at first. I love me. Hope no one is looking. *I love me.* The flow of love can now go in a direction other than toward me. Outward toward you. I mean that with precision: *you.* I love you.

I am responsible for my own world. How I feel is up to me. Since I now love me, no one can or has ever hurt me.

"There is no empty feeling, no place where my power goes out. All the power is kept inside." Love flows out and in like an inner tube around my heart.

I can forgive all if I can forgive myself. All experience is valid and therefore blessed.

Enter the echo of the helix drum
Opening multiple dimensions.
Like the stupa mirrored in the lake.
How great is life! Life is great.
The portal is wide open.

A Japanese Buddhist priest in Hawaii once described our lives as standing on a five-yen coin that has a hole in the center. Everyone stands on a different place on the coin, but we all have one leg dangling over the hole. As we go through life, we keep all our weight on the leg standing on the coin. Of course it gets tired and painful. This is suffering, disappointment, despair, and death. But all you need to be free from suffering is to shift your weight.

Over Sole

How clever of God to make me
With all of this beauty around
I shall keep on enjoying whatever I see
I'm the reason my blessings abound.

I was feeling great. The doc came in with good news. My blood count indicated that I was exceptionally healthy. Not in the least bit diabetic, they finally realized, and no trace of cancer. What? None? All this time I thought cancer would kill me. What a waste of time and energy. I feel like an iguana biting his tail. I can now leave that worry behind me.

News about my leg was not so good. We had brought blood back to the foot too late. The chances of saving it were very slim.

Take the ride that's given.

I asked for a wheelchair and wheeled myself out onto a balcony where I could be alone. I looked right at the sun and, blinking in the brightness, took a deep breath, went wide-angle into the moment, and said out loud to any powers in the universe I could will into being:

"Thank you. I don't know why you are doing this, why it is necessary for me to lose my foot, but I am no longer afraid. I love this life. I'll play the hand I have been given. Thank you, because I can see that all my life you have been giving me everything I needed for whatever I wanted to do. I want to see how you are going to turn this one into a blessing. You're being challenged, you know."

Stars When the Sun Shines

"Thank you" is how we sign the receipt when we are sent a blessing so that the delivery can be verified. Makes sending the next blessing easier.

And then I broke into a gospel song I had learned in high school chorus and never understood: "Sometimes I'm up, sometimes I'm down. Oh yes, Lord! Sometimes I'm bent almost over to the ground! Praise the Lord!"

Praise the Lord? Yes. I was feeling very emotional, and a wee bit theatrical.

We flew back to Thailand to have the amputation. It was one-tenth the cost, and we were without insurance, which wasn't available for someone with my medical history and lifestyle. I figured the universe would provide.

I flew back to Thailand for another reason. After I agreed to love myself, the separation between me and others faded. People related to me on a deeper level. Loving them without judgment allowed me to feel their joy and also their pain. Most nurses and doctors were in a lot of pain, and many had hidden their soul in a dark corner of their unconscious.

While I was still at Queens Hospital, nurses, especially, started coming to my room on their time off just to chat. Sympathy for my situation was prohibited in my room. It would tarnish my thank-you to the universe.

I had to send one nurse outside to be by herself to cry for a while. She couldn't have done it in front of a patient, or she could have cried in my room. I knew that the medical staff at Queens—with the present system based on drugs and insurance claims—no matter

Over Sole

179

how well meaning, were not going to be able to give me the care I would need to walk again after the operation. I was a project. I was down to 135 pounds, what I weighed when I was fourteen years old. I used to play football, a lineman. Was that the same person? It all appears as in a dream.

Was I the same person? When I left Queens Hospital, the staff was waiting in a smiling line to see me on my way. The same thing happened when we got off the plane for a layover in Japan, with the stewardesses and stewards waving and smiling, and again when we deplaned in Thailand—a row of smiling faces loving me in my wheelchair. When I went into a room, people turned golden. Smiles everywhere. Why hadn't I seen them before? Probably because I wasn't smiling.

The only reason you are being laughed at and not with is that you aren't laughing.

In Thailand people are more in touch with their spirit, probably because they have been unable to get in touch with so much money. There, I was confident that the entire burden of my recovery would be shared by friends and not fall entirely on Mars. I first contacted a healer in the hope that perhaps we could bring back some of these beautiful feelings to the three-dimensional world of my blackened foot. I was hoping this was all the result of a bad attitude we could correct. Perhaps I could miraculously get my foot healed. All you need to do is ask, and then forget about it. Only I couldn't forget about it.

Mor Nit tried her hardest. Her massages were painful. Still, I would not use pain pills. The ones I had been given in the hospital came close to killing me by causing a stomach ulcer. I had been rushed back to the hospital emergency ward for a transfusion, very near death.

I became adopted into Mor Nit's family. It was decided that the name Wayne was unlucky. They gave me a new name, Jahn. Ironically, I had been called John Wayne by the Portuguese Malaccans because of my "cowboy" lifestyle: I was living by my own rules, hitching up and down the Malayan Peninsula, no job, no schedule, free. Now I was to be called Jahn in a different culture for entirely different reasons. *Jahn* was short for *achan,* meaning "teacher." They called me teacher.

I didn't want to share my pain with anyone, but I do not have the tolerance to be a stoic. I couldn't take it anymore and cried out. *"Oh!"* But instead of stopping there I continued into a song: *"What a beautiful morning."* It helped control the pain. I remembered from my training in Kyōgen how I had channeled pain in my leg into power in my voice, and I decided to sing with a full throat as loud and on key as I could manage.

Kyōgen. The play I had been in was entitled *Sore Leg.* I had pretended onstage to have the very malady I was experiencing for real thirty years later in the same left leg.

I sang to channel the pain. The vibration I was sending into my body had a healing energy. Mor Nit's family came over to enjoy my musical massages.

Over Sole

My ulcer opened up again. I was rushed to emergency in Thailand and given copious quantities of Thai blood. To our adopted family, this made me even more Thai. The nurses and even some doctors lined up again, smiling and waving, as I left the hospital. I love them.

Mor Nit reluctantly admitted she was unable to pray me back to health. She asked if I would please visit the *wat,* the Thai Buddhist temple, with her. I went to please her. I was wheeled down the back alley of the *wat,* past monks lying around after they finished their daily morning meal. No meals in the hot afternoon when movement was slow. I was the movie of the day.

We arrived at a small, dark room near the back of a labyrinth of buildings. It was filled with crutches, children's toys, wigs, silk cloth, Thai masks, golden bowls, silk flowers. This hodgepodge of strange gifts surrounded a small statue of Buddha. I offered my personally hand-carved cane to the menagerie. I was hoping I would have no need of it.

An old monk entered. He asked me to lie down on my back with my head facing in the direction he indicated, pointing with his lips. My whole body was covered with a white cloth. White is the Asian color for death. He chanted a sutra in a low droning voice. I believe it was my funeral!

After he finished, I was asked to sit up, to turn facing the other direction, and then to lie down once more. I was again covered, this time with a red cloth. Red is the color for long life. He started chanting again and pouring copious amounts of water over me. I was being baptized. Does this make me a born-again Buddhist?

After that I went to a beautiful boutique hospital where they had a hyperbaric chamber. It felt great to experience that glass casket filled with an oxygen-rich atmosphere under pressure. I felt young again, optimistic like a spring morning running down a hillside barefoot in the grass. It did not, however, cure the foot.

On the day of the surgery, minutes before I was put to sleep, a nurse came hurriedly to me. Déjà vu. What now? They had forgotten to ask me: What did I want done with my foot? Was it OK if it was burned?

I said of course. Seemed a strange question. Do some people ask to take it home as a souvenir? *"I think I'll have mine bronzed."* They informed me that the only places in Thailand that have incinerators are the crematoriums at the *wats* and that the monks would likely be saying a prayer over it. Was that OK?

I said sure. I was finally getting a leg up on everyone. I am aware now of my over sole. From now on, I would be sure to get off on the right foot. I probably would have continued, but the anesthetics finally took effect, and I fell asleep.

The next day the surgeon came in to dress my wound. It was a painful process, so I naturally began singing. I chose at random: "I left my heart in San Francisco . . ."

Over Sole

When I came to the end, the Thai surgeon spread his arms theatrically and sang along with me, ". . . your golden sun will shine for me."

He had studied medicine in the States and loved to listen to the older songs; he could more easily understand the English lyrics.

The following day he returned to change the dressing once more. Instead of bracing me for pain, he asked me what song I was going to sing that day. I had chosen "Misty."

Look at me,
I'm as helpless as a kitten up a tree.
Never knowing my right foot from my left—

I stopped.

"You know, Doc. By now it should be obvious, don't you think?"

The doc and I became great friends. We would sing together every time I had a check-up appointment. When it was no longer necessary to visit him, he was a bit disappointed. "I will miss you, Jahn."

"I got a solution, Doc. Just audition your patients so you can keep on singing."

It took two months before I was fitted for my new foot. Our visa ran out. Mars applied for an extension on medical grounds and was given only three days. I wondered if, had I had both legs amputated, they would have given us six.

Stars When the Sun Shines

Anger or disappointment was not an option. Mars suggested we travel from Thailand up to Laos for our first trip there, me with only one leg and riding around in a wheelchair pushed uphill by her. She loves to travel. It was a great trip. I love the city Luang Prabang and the people there.

Patience is only an issue if it is missing. A friend of mine was in a motorcycle accident in rural Wyoming. He had to be helicoptered to the hospital. His body was broken, but not his intense, impatient spirit. On the day he was finally able to walk again, he went downtown, bought a ten-dollar watch, took it to the jewelers, and asked how much they would charge to remove the minute and hour hands. He was told that they would kick his sorry butt out of there for wasting their time with such foolishness unless he could give them a good reason for his request. If he could, they would do it for free.

"I've been watching the minute hand crawl for six months and it takes an eternity for an hour to pass. I don't ever want to know what time it is again. I just want to see the second hand move so I know I am still alive."

When I Walk Again
I'll stand up to cook our meals,
to write a poem,
to carve the image of a person standing.
I'll move my whole body
with the music of doing

Over Sole

When I walk again.
I'll marvel at the magic of placing
     one foot in front of the other,
          I'll glory at each and every step I make
               and all that happens as I pass
                    song of a bird,
                         swaying trees in a breeze,
                              floating clouds,
When I walk again.
I'll wink at the bright eye in the sky
     enjoying our shared secret
          as the sun journeys across the heavens,
               and I, too, in heaven
When I walk again.
I will dance,
     move both my feet
          to the rhythm in the air,
               move in unison with others in love,
                    dance a moving prayer of thanks
When I walk again.

I had been in a wheelchair for half a year, and I was tired of looking up at everyone my age but loved being level with children. I was uncomfortable with people walking and talking behind me. I wheeled myself on mile-long hikes, with Mars walking beside me. She'd cover me if I tired. We rolled along trails near our garden cottage located in a quiet golf resort north of Bangkok. Mor Nit had worked there before as a caddy and arranged for us to have our own private bungalow. She brought in our meals. We became friends with the staff and practiced speaking Thai with them.

The day of my final foot fitting, I put on a new bright purple silk Thai shirt with gold embroidery for the occasion. When I came out of the taxi upon our return, I stood and walked as if I were balancing on a tightrope. The staff was all smiles. They had only seen me wheelchair bound. I was beaming with joy.

Someone smiled and said, "Nice shirt!"

tMpL n 4st
temple in forest
....

SISYPHUS LOOKS AT HIS BOULDER, his eternal burden, as it careens once again down the hill. He takes a deep breath and smiles broadly. He looks up at the sky and says, "Thank you, God, for I have a reason for living." And with head held high he strides broadly down the mountain, enjoying his freedom. Life is good.

We can thank Albert Camus and Fred Nietzsche for this story.

Mine had been a grand, high-scoring pinball game that would win me more games if I had wanted them. Yet now I find that my silver ball has passed through the center of the flippers, right down the center and the only way out of the game.

The ball rolls away from the machine and comes to rest in a circle with other silver balls like mine, shining and hard, with a source of light hanging overhead and slightly above. Each ball reflects this light and also the light reflected from every other ball, every ball reflecting every other ball ad infinitum. Everything is lined up with everything. Everyone is reflecting everyone. Everything is contained in everything. The part is the whole. It is a hologram.

Wait a minute. This metaphor limps. It is way too two-dimensional. Let us pass through.

The outside of my silver ball softens in the warmth of self-love
   turning itself inside out with ease, becoming a translucent crystal.
   A gold light shines from within.
   I look at a dome above
   reflected in a dome below.
   The wall of this sphere is made of choirs of crystal balls the same as mine,
      each with its own golden glow
      radiating from within,
      each reflecting everyone
      and everyone reflecting each.
      The hollow hallowed hologram
      is centered on my heart,
      a torus of ever-circling energy

like an inner tube floating
on a milky river of stars.
This is creation and I am.
I co-create all.
Everything consists entirely
Entirely of
Love-consciousness.

tMpL n 4st: temple in forest

About the Author

....

Actor, writer, sculptor, humorist, teacher, husband, and world traveler, Wayne Stier's mission in life was to be aware—of where he was, what he saw, who he met, and whatever he was doing. He published three previous books and numerous magazines articles. He lived with his wife, Mars Cavers, in Ocean View, Hawaii.

To Our Readers

··

WEISER BOOKS, AN IMPRINT OF RED WHEEL/WEISER, publishes books across the entire spectrum of occult and esoteric subjects. Our mission is to publish quality books that will make a difference in people's lives without advocating any one particular path or field of study. We value the integrity, originality, and depth of knowledge of our authors.

Our readers are our most important resource, and we appreciate your input, suggestions, and ideas about what you would like to see published. Please feel free to contact us to request our latest book catalog, or to be added to our mailing list.

Red Wheel/Weiser, LLC
500 Third Street, Suite 230
San Francisco, CA 94107
www.redwheelweiser.com